BERYL WILLIAMS and SAMUEL EPSTEIN are husband-and-wife authors who sometimes write under the name of Douglas Coe, sometimes Martin Colt. Doing this book was the most fun of all, for it meant meeting several magicians who knew Houdini, and learning a lot of magic themselves.

7. 0~~,000,00~~ 70,000,000
                          20

        10,000
         1,000
    ──────────
    1,400,000

THE GREAT HOUDINI

BERYL WILLIAMS
SAMUEL EPSTEIN

SBS SCHOLASTIC BOOK SERVICES
New York Toronto London Auckland Sydney

Copyright 1951 by Beryl Williams and Samuel Epstein.
Copyright 1951 by Pocket Books, Inc. This edition is
published by Scholastic Book Services, a division of
Scholastic Magazines, Inc., by arrangement with Julian
Messner, Inc., and Pocket Books, Inc.

14th printing . . . . January 1971

Printed in the U.S.A.

Foreword

It is difficult to realize that someone you have known personally has become a legend, particularly when your recollections of that man are as vivid as yesterday's. Yet when I look back on my association with Houdini, the thing does not surprise me. Even during his lifetime, Houdini had created a certain aura about his name, if not himself. It was a logical sequence that one should be transcribed to the other, after his untimely death.

To my mind, the enigma of Houdini resolves itself into one question. Which was the more remarkable: the Houdini he wanted the public to believe in; or the Houdini he believed he was?

In this book, the authors have met that question fairly and directly. They have recaptured the spirit not only of Houdini's times and surroundings, but of the man himself. Through the perspective of years, they have given Houdini and his work a sound and intelligent appraisal which they have woven into the fabric of an entertaining story. Indeed, the story is all the more entertaining because of its accuracy, which is not surprising when we realize that the subject was a man whose life itself belonged in the field of entertainment.

Times and trends have changed. Today, perhaps, Houdini's work would require a different type of appeal to capture public interest. That, too, is a fact which the authors of this biography have not overlooked. It is a proven fact, however, that Houdini won the public of his day. It is an almost equal certainty that he would have done the same with a public of any other period. He knew the formula that gained such results.

Houdini, as he wanted the public to know him, was a man of exaggerated exploits. He could never completely fictionize his achievements, because always—almost on call—he had to deliver a reasonable facsimile of anything which he claimed he had accomplished. Charting a course between the commonplace and the impossible, Houdini steered his career through a strange limbo of the improbable. Time has magnified his deeds, carrying his fame even beyond some of the claims he was hesitant to make.

I repeat that this book has perspective, which is the essential quality in any treatment of Houdini. It does not let Houdini's claims, his glamor, or the mystery surrounding his secrets deceive you. It was Houdini's business to deceive the public. Were he alive today, he would still be making it his business, but his approach to deception, as well as his expansion of the theme, was entirely legitimate.

Finding the key to Houdini is quite as difficult

as it was to find the keys to his handcuffs, when he was locked and manacled in a jail cell. Nobody ever found those keys and perhaps the key to the real Houdini is quite as elusive. Somewhere, though, in his youth, he gained a strong responsibility of public trust. Whether from his early training, his circus days, his observations of police and their weaknesses as well as their methods, it is difficult to say. In this biography, you will find mention of Houdini's booklet, "The Right Way to Do Wrong," which became a classic in the analysis of petty crime. It shows that Houdini was highly observant of the harm that could be foisted on the public through illegitimate deception.

To prevent such harm became a cause with Houdini. All through his life, he championed what he thought was right and perhaps because of his own intensity, became convinced that he himself could do no wrong. It is certain that he was willing to gamble everything to further whatever he considered just. His attacks on fraudulent spirit mediums, as detailed in this biography, stand as an example. It has been said that Houdini was campaigning for publicity, but it could have backfired and proved his ruin.

I have watched Houdini perform his "Water Torture" escape, where he was locked in a tank of water upside down. I have also seen him defy a platform of spirit mediums to meet him in open debate, before an audience of their own followers, who outnumbered Houdini's friends five hundred to one. Which was more dangerous, the water cell that he had tested or the fanatical, untried crowd, I could not say. As for Houdini, I doubt that he either knew or cared.

Houdini's make-believe was not imagination, unless it could be termed a practical imagination. He guessed what was around the next corner instead of picturing what lay beyond the horizon. As a result, he was more often right than wrong. The authors have very effectively stressed Houdini's use of the word "challenge" during his rise to fame. They show Houdini as more than just a man who believed in himself. Houdini believed in Houdini.

That was proven by a later episode—ably related in this volume—when Houdini had a set-to with Jess Willard, the world's heavyweight champion. By then, Houdini, by dint of accomplishment, regarded himself a champion in his own right. Of what, he did not specify. He was Houdini. That was sufficient and he sold the public on the idea.

Once a rabbit escaped behind the scenes and got loose on Houdini's stage. Assistants were chasing it behind Houdini's back and the audience began to laugh. Turning around, Houdini saw the trouble; instead of being chagrined, he told an assistant to bring the rabbit to the footlights. There, Houdini seriously introduced the rabbit as the world's largest bunny, brought from Australia especially for his show. The audience applauded and Houdini solemnly bowed the rabbit off.

At the same theater where that occurred, I saw Houdini in his dressing room backstage, admiring a new trick that an amateur magician was showing him, and having his secretary take notes so that he, the Great Houdini, could practice the trick for himself. Perhaps it was those elements: the ability to rise to an occasion, the constant desire to learn more magic, that made Houdini great.

Such incidents show at least the human touch which motivated Houdini's career. You will find it apparent in the early chapters of this biography, with its thread persisting until the night of his final performance. A fabulous story, that of the Great Houdini, the more amazing because it is so human.

WALTER GIBSON

List of
ILLUSTRATIONS

The Great HOUDINI

Magician
Extraordinary

For more than a quarter of a century—from the year 1900 until his death in 1926—Houdini's name appeared, day after day, in newspaper headlines that were the envy of all his fellow-performers in the world of vaudeville:

HOUDINI, HANDCUFF KING, ESCAPES POLICE
FETTERS
THOUSANDS SEE HOUDINI TRIUMPH OVER
CHALLENGER
THRONG AWED BY WIZARD OF ESCAPE
HOUDINI AGAIN THE BIG MYSTERY

His life had, in the press, the recurrent thrills of a spectacular serial story. Over and over again, Houdini, the courageous hero, met the experts' challenges and overcame them by what seemed superhuman means—by means that some of his admirers believed to be quite literally superhuman.

Scotland Yard had declared that no man could escape from its shackles: Houdini slipped off a pair of Yard handcuffs as if they had been rubber bands. The Washington, D.C., jail that had imprisoned Guiteau, President Garfield's assassin, held Houdini for only a few moments. Bound by ropes and chains, locked into a heavy packing case, and lowered over the side of a ship into icy water, he emerged free and unharmed. He couldn't be restrained. Audiences all over the world hailed the skill of the Elusive American, as he was often called, and police authorities proclaimed their relief that Houdini had not decided upon a life of crime. As a criminal, they said—and the headlines quoted them—Houdini would have been difficult to catch and impossible to hold.

Houdini's career coincided roughly with the life-span of early vaudeville itself—developing before the turn of the century, and lasting until motion pictures replaced live performers in most theaters. He was a child of vaudeville, and one of its masters, especially skillful at the techniques of publicity that P. T. Barnum had first developed in pre-vaudeville days—techniques which vaudeville took over for its own, and which the movies later exploited to such extravagant lengths.

During his lifetime his name was a household

word. It appeared, in fact, in one of the standard dictionaries of the period: to *Houdinize* was "to release or extricate oneself (from confinement, bonds, and the like), as by wriggling out." There were those who claimed that this rare honor had been accorded the performer for not entirely honorable reasons—that a Houdini press agent had influenced one of the dictionary's editors. Houdini would probably not have scorned the distinction even so. Whatever the origin, he was quick to quote the definition in the colorful souvenir booklet, "The Adventurous Life of a Versatile Artist," for sale at all his performances.

Today, however, though his name no longer appears in our dictionaries, it remains indisputably in our language. Even as these pages were being written, it was overheard at a soda fountain, spoken from a motion picture screen, and used in a newspaper headline. We still call a brilliant football player a "Houdini" when he skillfully evades opposing team members. We say a politician has "done a Houdini" when he slips out of a tight corner.

So perhaps it is no longer very important to know whether Houdini was, as his enemies claimed—and he had many enemies—a performer whose chief ability was the one to publicize himself; or whether his admirers were right when they insisted that the headlines were tributes honestly won by a man whose ability to open locks, to free himself from almost any known restraint, was beyond imitation and close to genius. Perhaps the most we can learn from their arguments is that Houdini was the sort of man over whom such violent disagreements could arise.

He was in many ways a contradictory figure. Volatile and quick-tempered, he was at the same time cold-bloodedly unswerving in the further-ance of his career. He was selfish and suspicious as an artist—but his devotion to his mother was deep and real; his private and unknown philan-thropies were as numerous as those the press re-ported. He was generous to young performers—and bitter, sometimes cruel, to those who threat-ened his own position.

He waged unceasing war against those who in-sisted that they created their "magic," and against spiritualists who claimed to call forth the voices and spirits of the dead by other than purely phys-ical means—but he carried with him to the grave certain of his own secrets, and he dreaded ex-posure of his own tricks more than he feared any other one thing. "It was a trick," he would say; "I did it by purely physical means." But his explana-tion went no farther than that; and if many re-fused to believe him and credited Houdini himself with psychic or nonphysical powers, he left them to wonder—and to return to see him time and time again. A large part of his success lay in the fact that it was seldom enough to see Houdini once: whole audiences were composed of those who had paid to see him for the second or twentieth time, their wonderment only increased by the repetition, their curiosity still unsatisfied. "How does he do it?" was the formula for the constant word-of-mouth advertising that preceded and followed him wherever he went.

There is no doubt that Houdini thrived on the controversies that raged around him; that he even —his admirers and detractors alike attest to this— encouraged them. They made good copy. And, skillful or not, no public performer can survive without public notice. The many headlined stories that appeared about Houdini, once he became famous, are in themselves both source material and a source of confusion to us today. Are they fact or press agent's fancy; the truth about Houdini or what he wanted the world to believe? The question cannot always be answered with any certainty. We can learn a good deal about the exploits of the man who called himself Houdini. We can never be sure how much we know about the man whose real name was Ehrich Weiss, once he —and the world—had established him on a pinnacle as the Handcuff King. Perhaps the headlines conceal as much as they reveal.

Certainly he was a vigorous personality, with a remarkable physique and an equally remarkable knowledge of his own field. Certainly his curiosity about all things, and especially about all things "magical" and mechanical, was as real and eager as the public's curiosity about him. Envied and disparaged, hated and almost worshipped, flamboyant and reticent, he was representative of the whole gaudy era of vaudeville, when stars arose overnight in a blaze of publicity, and died as quickly the moment they lost the public's attention. Houdini failed to be representative of his time and his world only because he himself never relinquished his public once he held it in his hand.

He escaped from almost every kind of cell and fetter man could devise. He has not yet escaped from our minds.

2

From the moment young Ehrich Weiss saw the first magnificent posters for Jack Hoeffler's Five-Cent Circus, he knew he had to see the circus itself. He couldn't afford a ticket, of course. There was no money in the family for such frivolities. But the afternoon of the day the circus opened in town, he and several other boys—none of them was more than seven or eight—slid daringly under the ropes and stood up on the far side in a spellbinding field. The others rushed eagerly forward—they had all seen circuses before—but

Ehrich stood just inside the barrier, too wonder-struck to move.

The dusty, trodden grass beneath his feet might have been a golden carpet, each shoddy booth the brilliant background for a miracle. Here was everything he had ever dreamed of—all the beauty and excitement that he had somehow known must exist somewhere in the world.

The gray-blue eyes, set deep beneath a wide forehead and a shock of black curly hair, stared unblinkingly. The small stocky body shivered inside its hand-me-down clothes.

There—on the right—were an acrobat and his lady, both dressed from head to toe in pink tights that glittered with spangles. And they moved like gods—treading with glorious casualness a precarious path in the air marked only by the thinnest of wires, landing in their net with a high bounce that they transformed into a breath-taking somer-sault.

There—on the left—was an enormous fat lady, majestic in sequin-splattered satin. And beside her stood a man so tall and so thin that you could watch—with an amazement that was close to terror—the way his bones moved beneath his skin.

There was a lion in his cage. He was lying very still in a corner, his eyes half closed. But Ehrich had read about lions. He knew how wild they were: the lion was the king of the jungle. At any moment this one might spring, his forepaw flash

8

savagely through the bars. It would be wise to retire to safety. Wise, yes—but not valorous. Ehrich held himself rigid, and looked steadily into the lion's cruel face. This was the way brave men faced danger.

Long moments went by, and the lion remained motionless. It was Ehrich who moved, finally, and he moved with a swagger. He had frightened the beast into submission, by his calm, cool courage. Now he could set about exploring this wonderful new world of the circus, because he had explored his own courage first and found it strong enough to bear the weight of his fright. He would not fear to walk on that thin wire, now, or to—

Ehrich stopped dead, his swagger gone.

Before his very eyes something magical had happened! He—Ehrich Weiss—had seen it. A huge bouquet of flowers had been created out of nothing—by magic! One moment there had been an empty silk hat in a man's hand—and the next moment the flowers were being lifted out of it.

As if pulled by a magnet Ehrich moved closer to the platform banded by a huge banner that said: THE GREAT MERLIN. On the platform stood the Great Merlin himself. He looked like an ordinary man. He smiled and spoke like anyone else. But he took a handkerchief from his pocket—an ordinary handkerchief—shook it, folded it up, unfolded it again—and there was a deck of cards inside!

It couldn't possibly have happened. But Ehrich had seen it!

And then the Great Merlin spread the cards into a fan, passed his hand across them—and they had changed color from red to green!

Ehrich's heart was pounding. Certainly, he thought, nothing like this had ever occurred before outside of story books. There were magicians in story books, of course, along with witches and elves and ghosts and hobgoblins. But this one was alive and real.

The Great Merlin smiled as he picked up a slender black cane. Casually he twirled it on his finger. Then the cane became still in his hands, and slowly, from the end of it, the magician began to draw forth a bright red ribbon. There were yards and yards of it. And then there was blue ribbon and yellow ribbon and green ribbon. If he had flung a rainbow across the sky, it could not have been more spectacular.

All around Ehrich people were pausing for a moment or two before the Great Merlin's platform, watching, applauding occasionally, and then moving on. Ehrich didn't even notice them. One man in the crowd said to his companion, over Ehrich's head, "This fellow's terrible. Can't hold a candle to that chap I saw in Milwaukee last year. Now, there was a slick performer!" If Ehrich had heard he might have turned on the blasphemer with both fists. But his ears, like his eyes, were closed to everything except the wonders taking place before him. He didn't hear his name being called when his friends were ready to go. They left without him, finally. "Guess he went long ago," one of them said. "He's always rushing home to help his ma."

The rest of the audience finally drifted away too, as the supper hour approached for the town of Appleton, Wisconsin. But Ehrich stayed rooted to his spot. The performer stopped abruptly as the last of the adults departed, sent a single bored look in Ehrich's direction, and then sat down with a weary sigh on the gilt chair beside his magic table.

Ehrich still didn't move.

The Great Merlin scratched his head and tipped the chair back. "Enjoy yourself, kid?" he asked.

Ehrich swallowed, speechless.

"'Smatter? Waiting for a rabbit?"

Ehrich found the voice he had been reaching for, somewhere far down in his throat. "I think you're—wonderful," he managed.

The front legs of the gilt chair hit the platform with a thud. The Great Merlin bent forward, smiling again. "You do, eh?"

Suddenly there was a shining silver quarter in his thin hand. The hand moved, twisting at the wrist more swiftly than lightning—and the quarter was gone!

Ehrich could hardly breathe; it had been done just for him!

The magician was very close now, stooping at the edge of the platform. "Want to see how it's done?"

Instinctively, Ehrich backed away. There were things ordinary people had no right to know. Perhaps—the sudden thought was far more terrifying than the lion had been—perhaps the Great Merlin was an evil magician, like the one he'd read about in—

"Watch close now. Here it is, see?" The quarter gleamed again between thumb and forefinger. "I'll do it real slow this time. I turn my hand around—like this." Ehrich didn't want to look, but he couldn't turn away. "See? And while I'm turning, I shove the quarter between my fingers. Now it looks like it's gone. Don't it?"

He held the hand palm forward. The quarter was indeed gone.

"And the other side." The quarter was not there either.

It was gone, as utterly and mysteriously as it had disappeared before.

But the Great Merlin turned his hand once more, only halfway this time, so that the side of it faced Ehrich. And the quarter was *there*, caught between the third and fourth fingers, extending forward above the palm. The wrist flicked quickly, and the coin shifted, coming now into sight on the other side of the hand. It no

12

longer showed on the palm side—but it was still *there!*

The truth struck Ehrich like a clap of thunder.

The coin had been there all along! Sometimes Ehrich had been able to see it, and sometimes he had not, but it had never really—not really—vanished. Ehrich had been blindly, humiliatingly fooled.

"Here—watch it again, bub. I hold it like this, see?"

The Great Merlin was not a *real* magician. He fooled people.

But wait; there was more to it than that. The Great Merlin thought he had *not* fooled Ehrich. That was why he was talking to him like this—because he thought Ehrich was so clever that he—alone out of all the crowd—had known that these were tricks.

"You look like a bright kid. Bet you could pick it up in no time if you tried. Looks like it's gone, don't it? But you and I know different." The Great Merlin winked.

Both of Ehrich's wide, bright eyes winked back. He had been invited to join the charmed and secret circle of those who knew the truth and who could themselves seem to make magic for more credulous folk.

"Here—you try it. Jump up on the platform here, so I can see if you do it right." The Great Merlin reached down his hand, and Ehrich took it

instantly. "That's the boy. Here you are. Now:
hold it like this."

Ehrich—the Great Ehrich, he was suddenly—
took the coin between his fingers. It was the most
important moment of his life. He had stepped up
out of the audience, had crossed the dividing line
to the performer's side of the stage. He would
stay there now forever.

But in the Weiss home early that evening, life
was going on as usual. Mrs. Weiss—small and
quiet, with the deep eyes and broad brow of her
son, but with a wide, firm mouth that promised
a serenity Ehrich would never possess—Mrs.
Weiss was putting a supper of plain food on the
kitchen table and rounding up her brood. One of
them was sent to bring their father from his
books: Rabbi Weiss would always rather read
than eat, they said. They were ready to sit down,
finally—the four older children and the baby,
Theo. Only Ehrich was missing.

Mrs. Weiss wasn't worried. Ehrich had a curious independence for a child of his age, and it
wasn't surprising that he should be off somewhere
on his own rather than playing with the others in
the yard. But she was curious. Ehrich was devoted
to her: he always did as she asked, invariably came
home when she expected him. It was unlike him to
be late for supper.

While she fed Theo she questioned the others

about their small brother. One of them said he had seen Ehrich early in the afternoon with several other boys. "Looked like they were heading out toward the circus," he added.

"But he couldn't have gone in; he had no money," said their father, his scholarly brows raised in surprise over the illogic of his son's suggestion.

"No, sir." But Nat avoided his father's steady gaze.

The Weiss family had arrived in the United States only a few months before Ehrich was born on April 6, 1874. And it often seemed to the older sons that Rabbi Weiss still lived in his Budapest study, apart from the realities of life. They knew that at home in Hungary he had been a highly respected teacher; but here in Appleton it was different. Here he was a stranger and ignorant of many things they themselves took for granted. Instinctively they protected him. In Budapest, the son of Dr. Weiss would of course not have gone to the circus if he had no money —would probably not have gone in any case. In Appleton, it seemed quite sensible to his sons to sneak under the ropes along with their friends.

"No, sir," Nat repeated.

By the time supper was over Ehrich still had not come home, and his father set out to search for him. He looked in all the likely places—at the grocery where Ehrich sometimes picked up a few pennies running errands, at the homes of several of the boys Ehrich knew—and then he tried an unlikely place.

It was there at the circus that he found his son standing between the knees of a shabby, hoarse-voiced conjurer. For several minutes Ehrich didn't even notice the black-clad figure below the platform; he was too busy practising the subtle maneuver by which a pea might be made to appear under any of three overturned walnut shells.

Dr. Mayer Samuel Weiss shook his head slowly. That look on Ehrich's face—that intense absorption—was the look one saw on the face of a dedicated scholar. Something had happened to Ehrich, he realized. And Rabbi Weiss was wise in the knowledge that events have their own ways of shaping a life; that once they have taken place, they can never be undone or ignored.

His own life was dramatic proof of that. Left a widower soon after his early marriage to Rosa Schillak, who sang at the Hofoper at Budapest, he had—he thought—settled down to a career of books and loneliness. But some years later he had been asked to undertake a curious mission: to use his gift for speech to plead the case of a young friend too shy to propose marriage to the girl he loved. Dr. Weiss was surprised, but too kind to refuse. When he called upon the lovely young Cecelia Steiner he took one look at her and—like

John Alden—knew that he was in love with the girl himself.

He presented his friend's proposal, however, and she listened. He knew almost at once that her reaction was unfavorable to the suit. She made that clear. She also made it clear that she admired the message-bearer more than the message he brought.

Cecelia was less than half his age. Her family was well-to-do, he was not. But that same night he wrote her a long letter, telling her all about himself and asking her to be his wife. Cecelia accepted. They were married in 1864.

Surely that had been an unexpected event that had shaped more lives than his own.

And there had been that other, less pleasant, one. Even now Dr. Weiss did not like to think of it. It was seldom mentioned in the family. But the children knew, vaguely, that some great catastrophe had impelled the move from Budapest to America. Unlikely as it seemed, their slender, almost fragile, father had apparently fought a duel to avenge—so it was said—a slander against his race. And—this seemed even more unlikely—it was his skilled opponent who had been fatally wounded. The book-loving rabbi had remained alive, but he was unable to go on living at peace in his old home.

Shortly thereafter his wife brought the children to Wisconsin, where she had relatives, and soon he was able to follow her. Their comfortable life had been torn up by the roots and transplanted to a strange land, where they were without background and funds and almost without resources—and all by a single event which no one could have anticipated.

That was the way life was: things happened, and afterward the whole world was changed.

"Ehrich," Dr. Weiss said gently. "It is time to come home now."

He made no attempt, as they walked back through the summer dusk, to scold his son for being late, or to argue about the reason. Something had happened. For good or for ill, an event had occurred that might turn Ehrich's life in a new and entirely unlooked-for direction. But the event was a fact and, therefore, beyond recall. Now one could only wait and see what its results might be.

3

Every spare minute after that day Ehrich practised his "tricks." "Look," he was always saying. "Watch me do this."

Little Theo—or Dash, as the family always called him—was a constantly admiring audience. Ehrich saw him multiplied by thousands—saw himself, like the Great Merlin, standing on a platform, wildly applauded, rushing home afterward to fling into his mother's lap the dollars he had earned. He would dress his mother in golden dresses and buy his father all the books he wanted.

But that was only a dream. As the weeks and months went by, Ehrich knew it would all take longer than he had at first thought. Those tricks had looked so simple when the Great Merlin performed them. But when Ehrich attempted them, something was likely to go wrong. He would drop the coin instead of making it disappear. Or Dash—ignorant young Dash—would say calmly, "I know where the pea is: under *that* shell." And under that shell it would be.

And even—Ehrich told himself—even if he could eventually teach his fingers to be nimble and swift enough, so many of the tricks demanded equipment he couldn't afford. Ehrich was aware now that the yards of ribbon that had poured forth from Merlin's cane had not been created out of nothing, nor were they the product of his own hypnotized imagination. They were yards of real ribbon, cunningly wound up and concealed within a specially-built cane. And both the ribbon and the cane cost more money than Ehrich could earn in a year of running errands at the grocery.

There were, he decided, easier and quicker ways of joining a circus. He might, for example, become a wire performer—like the handsome gentleman in the pink tights who had walked so casually through the air. So Ehrich practised on the clothesline—and fell with a bone-jarring crash.

The man in the pink tights had also hung by his teeth from the suspended wire; so Ehrich tried this stunt on the clothesline—and fell again, and broke five teeth into the bargain. No one had told him that professionals who hang from wires wear heavy rubber guards in their mouths.

But no matter how many times he fell, Ehrich went right on practising. If he failed the hundredth time, then perhaps—he thought—he might succeed the thousandth time. He would keep on trying.

And in the meantime he used his sharp eyes and his newly-stirred curiosity to find out how all things worked. He examined hooks and eyes, purse fastenings, every bit of mechanism he could put his hands on. The town dump yielded up a rich collection of broken articles that he took apart and ingeniously put together again.

He made intricate knots in a length of string and then timed himself to see how fast he could take them out. He ordered young Dash to bind him up in lengths of rope, and worked at them until he was free. He discovered how to unlock his mother's cake cupboard—and Mrs. Weiss discovered that he knew.

Day after day he practised his acrobatics and his rope-walking, finding a new pride in a strong body and the control he was learning to exert over his limber muscles.

The summer he was nine a wonderful thing happened: Jack Hoeffler's Circus came to town again, and when Ehrich boldly showed the manager his tricks and asked for a job—he got it! He was actually hired as a performer.

He probably did a simple wire act, which would have been quite unspectacular if he hadn't been so young. And Jack Hoeffler was probably publicity-wise, as well as generous, when he permitted a local boy to appear with his show in Appleton. But to the new-born *artiste*—Eric, the Prince of the Air, he called himself, and he was splendid in long red woolen stockings that *almost* looked like tights—it all seemed wonderful. The dream was beginning to come true.

When the circus prepared to leave town, he took it for granted that he would go along. His career was launched; there must be no turning back. But his parents had other views. Even his father had not objected too strenuously when his son made an undignified spectacle of himself on the vacant lot that had mushroomed into tawdry splendor; but that a nine-year-old child should leave home, and in such dubious company—that was another matter and not to be allowed.

Ehrich clamped his lips together and looked grim. He would go without permission, he thought. But then his mother smiled at him, and he knew he couldn't. She would be too hurt. Fame and fortune would simply have to be postponed for a while.

That same summer he got a new glimpse of what worldly success could mean. His understanding father took him as a compensating treat on a day's trip to Milwaukee. There they both witnessed a performance by Dr. Lynn, the famous English magician. And instantly Ehrich's ambitions soared. The five-cent circus no longer seemed the ultimate in glory. This, now, was what he aimed for: a solo performance in a great hall—dignified, magnificent, attended by obsequious assistants, and applauded by people who had paid much more than a nickel for the privilege of viewing the magician's wonders.

And these were indeed wonders. Ehrich's credulity flowed back at one moment, and he was almost convinced again that there was real magic: Dr. Lynn cut off a man's arms and legs— and then put them back together again! But after the first terrified gasp, Ehrich's inner voice reminded him that it was only a trick. Everything could be explained, he told himself, if one only knew enough.

Years later Houdini purchased that particular trick from Dr. Lynn's son and presented it as a humorous interlude in his own performance. The techniques of illusion had come a long way in the intervening years. Ehrich Weiss had come even further.

Back home again from Milwaukee, he began to search Appleton for books on magic and to devour the few he could find. It was difficult to purchase even those few with the pennies he allowed himself out of his earnings. Things were not getting any easier for the Weiss family. The teaching Rabbi Weiss could find to do, the rabbinical services he was occasionally asked to preside over, paid very poorly. And there was an increasing number of mouths to feed—six boys now, and a baby girl, little Gladys.

Ehrich sold papers and shined shoes. Once or twice again he held brief jobs with traveling shows. As Eric, the Prince of the Air, he walked the tightrope. As Eric the Great he allowed himself to be tied up in a confusing tangle of ropes and then—while the audience clucked in gratifying sympathy over the effort it cost him—he slithered and worked his way out of one bond after another until he was free.

Finally—more eager for money than for education just then, although he was to spend the rest of his life regretting the years of study he had missed—he left school for good and took a fulltime job. He went to work in a luggage shop. It was heavy work, lifting trunks all day and transporting them from one part of the shop to another. But studying the different kinds of locks with which the trunks were fastened was endlessly exciting. Before many months had gone by, Ehrich found a new job that better suited both his size and his interests: he was apprenticed to a locksmith.

Locks are nearly as old as civilization itself, and their intricacies are numerous. In Appleton, a fairly new town, less than thirty years old when

Ehrich was born, there was not a wide variety for him to practise on. The huge locks and keys, popular until the previous century, had already almost disappeared, and certainly did not exist on new-built houses.

The locks Ehrich became acquainted with were simple, modern, workaday ones. But they were enough for a beginning. Hour after hour he studied the principles by which the notches in a key manipulated the mechanism of a lock, and the differences between one type and another. Once he understood the principle he found that he could usually open a lock with a simple piece of bent wire. This amateur lockpick which he contrived for himself he carried everywhere, trying it on every new lock he encountered and changing its shape time and again to make it more versatile. Once he even had the chance to use it on a pair of police handcuffs, and to his enormous pride, it worked even there.

Altogether the apprenticeship was an excellent one for a boy with Ehrich's powers of concentration, his deft tinkering fingers, and his perpetual curiosity. He learned a great deal and enjoyed the learning.

But finally the day came when he felt Appleton had no more locks for him to explore. With a boy's cockiness, he thought he had outgrown the town—outgrown it in every way. He knew all the swimming holes along the Fox River, and the way its rapids dashed down over the rocks. But he had never seen an ocean. He had ridden on one of the town's new streetcars—there were five of them, operated by electricity. Even Chicago had had street cars for only three years. But those in Appleton, proud though the citizens were of them, didn't go out into the strange world beyond the town's limits, and more and more that was where Ehrich wanted to be. He wandered around the saw mills, the paper mills, the cabinet factory, and the flour mills—but none of them tempted him as places for a lifetime's work. They weren't exciting enough; they weren't glamorous enough.

The Weiss family belonged, Ehrich sometimes thought resentfully, in a big city where they would be honored and respected. Hadn't his father been a well-known scholar in Budapest? But here in Appleton they lived on a poor side street which was almost unknown except among the other immigrants like themselves. He would like to *show* the others that he was as good as—no, better than!—they were.

The applause that had filled the Milwaukee hall when Dr. Lynn performed there was still sounding in Ehrich's ears. He would like to have people applaud like that for him. Then people would regard his mother with the respect she deserved. "Look," they would say, "there is the mother of
26

the famous. . . ." Yes, famous. That's what he must be.

On his twelfth birthday he walked home from work more slowly and more thoughtfully than was usual. He had infinite confidence in himself. He felt certain that he could, somehow, make his way alone. He knew definitely that he wanted to try. But would his mother be upset if he ran away?

He felt responsible for his mother, and he knew she depended on him. Even his father knew it. That very morning he had said quietly to Ehrich, "My son, if anything should ever happen to me, I know that I can trust you to look after your mother." And Ehrich had nodded solemnly, and accepted the trust. How, under the circumstances, could he even consider leaving home?

Ehrich asked himself that question a thousand times during the next few weeks, and finally he worked out a satisfactory answer. It was true, he decided—just as he had told himself before—that he could never be rich and famous if he stayed at home and went to work in one of the mills. Therefore it was his duty to go out into the world. It was *right* to do what he wanted to do.

As soon as he had made up his mind, he acted. Early one morning, a few weeks after his birthday, he walked out of the Weiss house and out of Appleton. No one knew he was going, and he left no message behind. He wanted to be certain that he was safely beyond his parents' reach if they should try to bring him back.

It was a sunny spring day; he had no burden but the clothes he wore; and the taste of freedom was intoxicating. When he grew tired of walking he managed to get a ride on a freight train, and his heart beat faster as it carried him farther and farther from home—past blue Lake Winnebago, and on for long bright miles southward through rich flat farmland. By late afternoon he had reached the small town of Delevan, Wisconsin, well over a hundred miles from home—and he was extremely hungry.

He wasn't worried, though, as he swung down from his illegal perch. He could work. He didn't expect to be hungry very long. With considerable nonchalance he marched up to a pleasant-looking farmhouse and knocked on the door.

"How do you do?" he said politely to the woman who stood looking down at him a moment later. "I thought if you had some work, I could earn my supper."

"Did you indeed?" But the woman didn't laugh. Ehrich was so sober, so determined-looking despite his size, that she knew instinctively she dared not seem amused. "Why don't you come in and have something to eat now?" she suggested. "We can discuss the work later."

"Well—all right."

He tried not to let her know that the food

made him very sleepy—he'd been up so early that morning to make his secret departure. But somehow she seemed to realize it without being told.

"And why don't you lie down there by the fire and take a little nap?" she said when he had finished. "We'll still have plenty of time to talk about the work."

Ehrich woke up the next morning. His torn trousers had been miraculously patched in the night, and his dusty jacket had been brushed. Its pockets were stuffed with sandwiches and cookies.

When he set off down the road a little later, with a warm breakfast inside him, Ehrich knew he hadn't properly expressed his gratitude. He wasn't good at making pretty speeches. But he had found out that the woman's name was Mrs. Flitcroft, and he remembered it. He remembered it until, long afterward, he received the payment for his first full week's work as a performer; and then he bought a blouse, pinned a five-dollar bill to it, and mailed the present to Delevan, Wisconsin. Mrs. Flitcroft had treated him as his own mother might have done, and Ehrich could never forget anyone who reminded him of his mother.

A day or two later, convinced that he had been right in thinking he could make his way alone, he sent a postcard home. "Dear Ma," he wrote, "I am going to Galveston, Texas, and will be home

in about a year. My best regards to all. Your truant son, Ehrich Weiss."

He was, as he had promised, gone for about a year. And though he never got to Galveston, he did get to a lot of other places. Wherever he went he did odd jobs to earn his meals and a night's lodging. Sometimes he could pick up a few pennies by standing on a street corner and doing tricks. Occasionally he worked briefly with a small carnival or medicine show. He never had any hesitation about asking for such jobs. Holding himself as tall as possible, he would announce, "I am Eric the Great. I can let anyone tie me with ropes, and I can get free." Out of curiosity or boredom, managers usually gave him a chance. And more often than not they took him on when they had seen what he could do—not because they were particularly impressed with his performance, but because Ehrich was so serious about it they didn't have the heart to turn him away.

Once, when Eric the Great was performing with a small circus, the management attempted to add color to his act by having the local constable on hand to tie him up. And the constable joined generously in the applause when Ehrich freed himself. But then, thinking perhaps that he had been belittled in front of his fellow-townspeople, the constable added, "Here—you're such a smart youngster. Let's see you get out of these." And he pulled a pair of shining handcuffs out of his pocket, winking over Ehrich's head at the crowd.

"Well. . . ." Ehrich's hand slipped into his own pocket, as he hesitated, and there he found what he was looking for—what he knew he would find, because he carried it with him always. It was the tiny lockpick he had made during his apprentice days. Holding it tightly between his fingers, he looked up. "I'll try," he said steadily. "But not in front of everyone. You must let me get off by myself."

The crowd laughed, and continued to laugh as the handcuffs were clamped on. Ehrich was allowed to step behind a curtain—grinning volunteers stood guard to see that no accomplice joined him there—and a few minutes later he stepped out again. The handcuffs dangled, open, in his hand.

The crowd stared for an instant, and then burst into applause. It was the first time that any performance of his had won a really rousing burst of handclapping—to say nothing of the genuine amazement on the constable's face, which was perhaps the most flattering reaction of all. It occurred to Ehrich suddenly that if he owned a pair of handcuffs, and could offer himself regularly as a performer capable of escaping from these seemingly inescapable bonds—then indeed he might have an act that would make Eric the Great famous.

But handcuffs were expensive. It was the old story, Ehrich thought grimly: to do a really impressive performance, it was necessary to have impressive equipment. And he was a long way from being able to afford that as yet.

As he filled in the long waits between show jobs with all sorts of chores—running errands, carrying parcels, weeding gardens, doing whatever offered itself when he was in need of a meal or a night's bed—he sometimes felt that running away from home had been a mistake after all.

By the end of a long year he still wasn't famous and he wasn't rich—and he was already thirteen.

Just then a belated letter from home caught up with him, and Ehrich learned that the Weiss family was starting life all over again, in still another new place. This time it was to be New York.

The name had the same thrill for Ehrich that it has long had for so many young people. New York . . . it was the mecca, the center of everything, and especially of the world of entertainment. That's where Tony Pastor's was, and Barnum's great show place. New York was the most exciting of all exciting big cities, and—why, of course!—it was certainly the place for a great performer to become quickly famous.

Ehrich made up his mind. The next time he boarded a freight train it was headed eastward, toward the Atlantic coast.

4

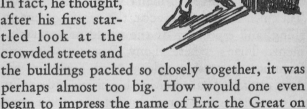

New York was indeed a big city, just as Ehrich had expected it to be. In fact, he thought, after his first startled look at the crowded streets and the buildings packed so closely together, it was perhaps almost too big. How would one even begin to impress the name of Eric the Great on all these busy, important-looking people?

But before he really faced the problem, he had to put it aside entirely. He discovered that it was only his father who had come on to New York. The rest of the family was waiting in Appleton until Dr. Weiss could send them the money for their fare. Ehrich settled down to help his father earn the necessary amount.

They were both poorly equipped for the task they had set themselves. Ehrich was young and inexperienced. And Dr. Weiss—though he knew German and French and Hebrew—knew almost no English. But the elderly scholar opened a small school for the teaching of Hebrew and the Talmud, and set himself—at sixty-four—to learning the language of his adopted country. Ehrich helped in the school for a time, but not very effectively. He had never troubled to learn much Hebrew himself and was scarcely a valuable assistant under the circumstances. After a short time he took a job as a messenger instead.

Now there was no money at all to spend on magic books or on anything else but the barest necessities. Ehrich and his father lived a frugal and lonely existence. But when the Weiss family was finally reunited again, in a crowded poorly-lighted flat on the upper East Side, Ehrich knew that the self-denial had been worthwhile. It was wonderful to see his mother once more—so wonderful that he could almost forget he had meant to be famous by their next meeting. And in any case the family seemed as proud of him as if he had really accomplished something during his year of wandering. Young Theo, comfortingly, looked up to Ehrich as a man who had seen the world.

It made Ehrich feel grownup and responsible, to be able to show his mother and his older brothers around the city. In keeping with his new mood he found a better job, joined the Allerton Club, where he made new friends, and gave every evidence of a boy who meant to settle down to be a solid, home-abiding wage earner.

Ehrich had become a tie-cutter. To his agile fingers and quick brain, the work seemed ridiculously simple. He was soon expert at it. But the new mood and the pride he took in his work didn't last. Soon Ehrich was reminding himself that cutting ties was not the swiftest road to fame and fortune.

He began to spend more time on his tricks again, and to borrow from the public library such fascinating books as Hoffmann's *Modern Magic*. He and Theo learned acrobatic stunts together, to strengthen and discipline their bodies, and practised with old decks of cards until they could imitate the easier card manipulations which Ehrich had seen the professionals perform. And when Ehrich joined the Pastime Athletic Club, then on 56th Street, he found new scope for his energies and his ambition. He became a skilled swimmer. He won a prize in a track meet, and had his picture taken in the handsome pair of red satin shorts his mother had made him for the event. He wasn't very tall—he was never to be more than five foot eight—but he was wiry and was becoming very strong. His pride in that strength remained with him all his life, and he was never to cease the regular and strenuous exercises which maintained his remarkable physical condition.

He also discovered, at the Pastime A.C., that he and Theo were by no means the only boys in the world who were interested in magic. One of the friends he made there was Joseph Rinn, the son of a well-to-do hotel manager. Rinn was several years older than Ehrich, and considerably better educated. But he and Ehrich found they had much in common. They both loved magic and athletics, and they shook hands on a youthfully solemn pledge to keep in training: neither of them, they swore, would ever smoke or drink so long as they lived—and neither of them ever went back on his word. It was Rinn who introduced Ehrich to a book which furnished them both with many hours of stimulation.

There was, at that period, a rapidly rising interest in spiritualism, the belief that the living can communicate with the spirits of the dead. All over the country "mediums" were claiming the ability to establish contact with what they called the Other World. Some were sincere people. Others were clever tricksters, deliberately producing "voices" and table rappings and other more dramatic manifestations for the terror and delight of an audience—and growing rich on the fees they collected from men and women eager to receive a message from beyond the grave. Mediums were to become much more numerous later, but even during the '90's they were widely popular, and already they were subject to the exposés of those who thought them harmful and dishonest.

The book Rinn showed to Ehrich was an exposure of the tricks that some of the fraudulent mediums used: it explained how, although bound hand and foot in the presence of witnesses, the medium could—under cover of the darkness always demanded for a spiritualistic séance—free himself in order to ring the bells, tap the tables, and contrive other "signs" of a spirit presence.

Rinn's curiosity about life-after-death had prompted his purchase of the book. Ehrich's own interest in it was chiefly aroused by the intricate rope-ties described, and by the methods that could be used to slip in and out of such bonds with great rapidity. Together the two boys studied the ties and practised them, until they both became adept at extricating themselves from the most difficult.

Gradually Ehrich was acquiring a small reputation among his friends as a conjurer. Inevitably the reputation resulted, one day, in his being asked to present some of his tricks at a program being planned by a neighborhood club. Ehrich accepted eagerly—and then grew frightened. This would be his first appearance on a New York stage and—however obscure the stage—he couldn't bear the thought that his performance might be less than impressive.

"I hate to go up there as Eric the Great and then just do a couple of simple old coin manipulations," he told Joe Rinn. "If I had some decent equipment, I could really show them something."

"Well, come on then," Rinn said. "We'll go to Martinka's and I'll stake you to some stuff."

Ehrich had often hung around the city's magic supply shops and had occasionally even bought a coin with two heads or an inexpensive deck of trick cards. But he had never had the chance to purchase real magical equipment before. He couldn't resist the offer. Later, like most men of his profession, he spent thousands of dollars on elaborate materials for illusions and other magical apparatus. But probably no purchases were ever so exciting as the ones he made that day from genial mustachioed Francis and Antonio Martinka.

The performance went off well. Solemn as always, but with a new arrogance born of knowing that he was working with real magical equipment, Ehrich successfully mystified his audience. The applause wasn't thunderous, but at least it was applause. And thereafter Ehrich, sometimes alone and sometimes with Theo, appeared frequently at the entertainments presented by a literary club or a local Friendly Society. Sometimes he even made a dollar or two out of these affairs, and the money always went for more equipment or for books on magic.

One of these books was *The Memoirs of Robert-Houdin, Ambassador, Author and Conjurer, Written by Himself*. Ehrich found it in a second-hand shop one evening on the way home from work, and sat down with it in his room right after supper. When his mother came in to wake him in the morning she found him sitting on the bed poring over its pages.

"You shouldn't get up early to read, son," she said. "You need your sleep."

Ehrich looked up vaguely. For a moment he scarcely recognized her. "Get up?" he echoed. And then the vagueness fled. "I didn't get up— I've been reading all night, Ma! And this is the greatest book in the world! Now I know what I want to do. I'm going to be exactly like this man. He was wonderful! He——"

"Ehrich, you'll be late to work," Mrs. Weiss said firmly. Ehrich was always making rather dramatic pronouncements about his future. Someone had to see to it in the meantime that he ate three meals a day and got regularly to his job. "Shame on you," she added, "sitting up all night!"

"But, Ma! He——"

"Ehrich."

"Yes, Ma." With an apologetic grin he followed her meekly out to the kitchen, but the book was in his pocket.

This was the real thing, he knew. Now his ambition had a focus and a design it had never had before. Even his father would be proud of him, he thought, if he could be a magician like the great Robert-Houdin. The famous Frenchman had always performed in faultless evening dress —never in the multi-colored costumes that had, until his time, identified conjurers with street fairs and circuses. His dignity had lifted the make-believe of the itinerant fakir to the glorified heights of an art and a profession. Robert-Houdin had performed before royalty, at the invitation of kings.

In the palace at Saint-Cloud once, for example —Ehrich had read that passage half a dozen times —Robert-Houdin had borrowed six ladies' handkerchiefs, made them vanish into the air, and then asked a fascinated King Louis Philippe to name the place where he wished the handkerchiefs to reappear. The King had decided upon the chest at the foot of the last tree along one of the garden walks. Robert-Houdin had nodded, led a procession of the guests to the spot named, waited calmly while workmen dug around the roots of the tree, and smiled at the guests' amazement when the shovels struck against an old iron-bound box. The King himself opened the box— and there they were: the handkerchiefs that the

magician had whisked into the air in the drawing
room some minutes before.

Robert-Houdin could cause an orange tree to
spring up out of a table, to burst into blossom
and leaf, and finally to put forth fruit—real
oranges, which he politely offered to his audi-

42

ence to eat. He possessed small doll-like automata, little figures of a girl, a pastry-shop owner, a wine seller, which at the wave of the magician's hand would write the answers to questions or serve whatever kind of sweets and wine his guests commanded.

But the most wonderful thing about the book was not the suavely romantic personality of Robert-Houdin himself, nor the marvelous performances he described; it was the fact that the conjurer-author told *how* his effects were achieved: how the intricate little automata were mechanically contrived in such a way that they would respond to his commands, how the orange tree was made to grow up out of the table by a complicated system of tiny air pipes manipulated by a hidden assistant. Clearly, and with a mechanic's accuracy, Robert-Houdin explained many of the devices which he had himself, he wrote, invented.

Surely, Ehrich thought, working halfheartedly at his cutting table that morning, Robert-Houdin had been truly a great artist. He, Ehrich, would be just such a man.

And then he looked down at the yards of material spread out below his hands, and wondered with distaste what he was doing in an ugly and unromantic tie factory. He would give up his job, he decided, and never waste another moment at the dull pursuit of merely making money. Of course he intended to make money—quantities of it. But he meant to make it at his chosen profession. He, too, would be applauded by kings and presented with medals testifying to his greatness. He, too, would write books.

Ehrich talked it all over with his friends. Joe Rinn was by no means convinced that Ehrich could make a success of conjuring. Ehrich wasn't, Joe thought, a very good showman—he presented his tricks too solemnly, too stiffly, to call forth the kind of audience enthusiasm that can create a beloved and successful performer. Joe suggested that if Ehrich was really convinced that he must do this risky thing he should at least obtain a letter of recommendation from his employer first. It was foolish, Joe pointed out, to burn one's bridges completely. Ehrich might want to be a tie-cutter again some day.

Jack Hayman, another friend, and one with whom Ehrich had given conjuring performances several times, responded more satisfactorily. He, too, had fond dreams of devoting his life to magic, and it seemed natural to him that Ehrich should plan to do so.

"I want to be just like this Houdin fellow," Ehrich said over and over, dropping half his hero's name out of ignorance rather than lack of respect. "I want people to say that Eric the Great is. . . ." Swiftly he turned to another facet of the endlessly fascinating future. "D'you think that's a good name, by the way? Eric the Great, I mean."

"I've got an idea!" Jack pointed to the book that lay open between them. "Why not take *his* name? I've heard that if you add an 'i' to a word, in French, it makes the word mean '*like* so-and-so.' So how about Houdin-i—'like Houdin'? The old boy was pretty famous. It wouldn't hurt to have people think of him when they hear a name."

"Houdin-i. Houdini." Ehrich repeated it over and over. "I like that," he said finally. It was another solemn moment, another dramatic pronouncement. "Yes—Houdini. That's it. Eric the Great—" Ehrich Weiss waved his hand in the classical gesture of vanishment.

Eric the Great immediately disappeared, and with him went Ehrich Weiss. It was Houdini who sat there, looking ahead down the years. It was Houdini who loftily informed his employer that he wouldn't be able to work for him any more— although it was the last lingering trace of Ehrich Weiss who recalled Joe Rinn's advice and asked for a letter of recommendation before he left.

The letter said, "To whom it may concern: We hereby certify that Mr. Ehrich Weiss has been in our employ for two years and six months as assistant lining cutter and we cheerfully recommend him as an honest and industrious young man." Ehrich put the letter away—and Houdini forgot it.

"Honest and industrious. . . ." How dull the words sounded! He meant to go on being honest, of course, and he expected to be far more industrious than he had ever been before. But in every other respect his life would be changed. He was about to step out on a glittering path that would take him far from the tie factory, into royal palaces and gilded theaters . . . to fame and fortune.

"I am Houdini," he murmured to himself in the close dark of his small bedroom. "I am Houdini the Great . . . the *Great*."

5

With Jack Hayman, then with Jack's brother, Joe, and later with his own brother, Theo, Houdini spent the following months seeking desperately for opportunities to present the act he called The Houdini Brothers. His efforts were mostly unsuccessful. And the failures were particularly discouraging when the death of Rabbi Weiss, shortly after the new career was launched, left Houdini with an increased sense of responsibility for his family and especially for his mother. But he refused to give up and return to the tie factory. He meant to fulfill his pledge to his father, but he meant to do it in his own way.

With the intention of appealing to a variety of tastes, Houdini included in their act a little of everything. His repertory now included simple magic tricks, card manipulations, and two

47

items he was particularly proud of: one was a handcuff release—he had at last managed to buy a pair of handcuffs; the other he called the trunk trick, and it utilized a trick box he had purchased from a down-and-out magician.

The handcuff release didn't impress people very much. For one thing, Houdini was not the only performer who did it; there were numerous handcuff artists in existence by the time he entered the ranks. Houdini was convinced that none of them had his own intimate knowledge of locks and that most handcuffs were fakes which could be opened by pressing a hidden spring. And although audiences apparently agreed with him, they unfortunately seemed to include Houdini in their judgment.

But the trunk trick, also an old one, was far more effective—almost as effective as Houdini's grandiloquent title for it: "Metamorphosis." The trick had drama and surprise: Houdini, his hands tied behind his back, would step inside the trunk, his partner would lock him in, bind the trunk with heavy ropes, and then pull a pair of curtains shut before it, stepping back behind the curtains himself just before they closed. Almost immediately thereafter Houdini would step out from between the folds, his hands free. With a dramatic gesture he would pull the curtains open to reveal the trunk still securely bound, and then he would untie the rope and lift the lid, and

Theo—or Jack or Joe—would rise from within it, *his* hands bound with the same tapes that had been on Houdini's. The first prisoner had been "metamorphosed" into the second.

Audiences liked it. Even if they suspected that there was a trick to the trunk itself (part of one side could be let down from within, permitting easy entrance and exit without touching the locks or ropes), they realized that a good deal of skill and agility was required to make the shift so quickly. But when Houdini followed the trunk trick with card manipulations they had seen before, with production of the same old ribbons and flowers they had watched magicians produce for years, with the handcuff release, their interest lagged. Houdini couldn't understand it: some of the card stunts were far more difficult to perform than the trunk trick, and his handcuff release was done with regulation cuffs. He was determined that one day the work he considered to be his best should be recognized, but he didn't know how to demand that recognition.

During the year following their father's death, he and Theo drifted westward, barnstorming as they went; performing in schools, at firemen's benefit carnivals, on street corners, wherever and whenever they could. Ehrich—or Harry, as he now called himself, because he thought it sounded better with Houdini—had come to the conclusion that New York was not after all the best place in which to inaugurate a performer's career—at least so long as New York remained blindly unaware of the performer's gifts. By the time they reached Chicago, the great World's Fair of 1893 was in progress there, and they managed to obtain a job in a side show. It was a fairly good job. While it lasted their hopes rose swiftly. But when the Fair was over they were once more merely another pair of youthful magicians out of work. Finally Houdini, by himself this time—Theo returned home—was hired by Kohl and Middleton's Dime Museum.

There was a dime museum in almost every sizeable town in the country in those days, and they all shared one great drawback in most performers' opinion: they required from a dozen to twenty shows a day, from ten in the morning until ten at night. But in Houdini's eyes this strenuous regime was pure pleasure. He was perfectly willing to appear twelve hours a day on one of the little platforms in the Hall of Freaks and Miracle Workers, where all the acts worked simultaneously, like side shows in a circus; and, at intervals, to hurry downstairs to the theater section—most Dime Museums had both a hall and a theater—to do a new group of stunts for the several daily programs presented there. He had enormous vitality, and hard work never frightened him. He loved every minute of it.

Kohl and Middleton's show place in Chicago

was one of the better dime museums, and it paid regular, if meager, salaries. Every week Houdini could send home several dollars out of the twelve he earned. He could also, to his endless delight, watch all the other performers at their work. They all enchanted him—the sword swallowers, the jugglers, the strong men, the bearded ladies, and the fire eaters. He learned something from each, convincing himself over and over again that the most impossible-looking feat was possible, if one only understood the trick behind it. But the sword swallowers, the jugglers, and the strong men were his greatest idols: they had to have skill as well as the knowledge of their trade's secrets. Houdini had always a special admiration for those who shared his own pride in practised ability.

Most of the artists were glad enough to talk to an eager beginner. Only one of them snubbed him. Horace Goldin, a well-known magician filling Kohl and Middleton's headline spot, pointed out the difference between Houdini's salary and his own magnificent one of seventy-five dollars a week, and added that two performers of such different quality could have nothing to discuss. It was the kind of insult Houdini could never forget and never forgive. Years later he was still, at every opportunity, repaying Goldin bitterly for that rebuff. But Goldin was almost the only flaw in a happy and exciting period: Houdini the magician had become a reality.

He was reduced to picking up odd jobs in the outskirts of New York.

Unfortunately, however, although Kohl and Middleton had no complaint against Harry's work, their policy demanded a frequent change of program. Before long, Houdini found himself on the road, and by the following spring he was once more living with his family. Again he was reduced to picking up odd jobs in the outskirts of New York. He had learned for the first time the lesson he was to learn over and over: that one successful engagement does not make a performer's career, any more than one swallow makes a summer.

Some of his jobs were at beer halls, and these Houdini never much enjoyed. It was not only his own disapproval of drinking that made him inclined to look down on his audience in those places. It was also because beer hall customers often preferred their drinks and their own stolid or raucous conversation to the free entertainment presented on the tiny stage at one end of the room. Houdini was quick to take advantage of certain kinds of advice that came his way. Once a manager asked him why he said, "You can see, ladies and gentlemen, that I ain't got nothing up my sleeve."

"Why shouldn't I say it?" Houdini asked.

And when the older man explained that it wasn't good grammar, that "I have nothing up my sleeve" was the correct phrasing, Houdini thanked him briefly and dropped the offending phrase from his speech forever. But when beer hall owners suggested that Houdini "loosen up a little, be more friendly with the customers," this was advice he couldn't accept. He went right on presenting his act with as much dignity as cheap ill-fitting evening clothes permitted, hoping that he had at least something of the suavity of his hero, Robert-Houdin. He would make no concession to the noisy jollity of the beer hall, no effort to adjust his act to its own brand of spirited good humor. It was little wonder, perhaps, that the harder he tried to impress, the more bored his audiences became.

Sometimes he received the same kind of reaction in the music halls, where audiences and entertainment were of a similar loud and vulgar character. A music hall, or concert hall, might be any large room in a town, sometimes used for local club meetings, sometimes hired by a troupe of traveling performers or by a local manager who staged programs there. Blackface minstrel shows, acrobats, singers, monologists, were the population of the music hall stage, and laughter was their chief commodity. Harry Houdini had no laughter to sell.

Nevertheless, beer halls, music halls, and dime museums, together with traveling circuses and medicine shows, offered almost the only opportunities then available to performers. Alone, or with Theo, Houdini played them all—whether he liked them or not.

But that same spring an event occurred which resulted in Theo's being permanently dropped from Houdini's act. Houdini fell in love, and ten days later he acquired a wife and a lifelong partner.

Bessie—Beatrice Rahner—could speak German, which was the language the Weiss family commonly spoke among themselves at home. In almost every other respect she seemed the least likely wife in the world for ambitious young Houdini to have chosen. But his impetuous wooing of her, and the runaway marriage, had none of the ill effects that sometimes resulted when Houdini's heart overpowered his cool head. And Bessie's childlike agreement to the frivolous elopement—they were married in Coney Island, at the end of a giddy afternoon which they had spent in exploring the wonders of the famous resort's shows and "death-defying" rides—hardly suggested the sober sense of responsibility she soon evidenced. It was she, in the long years ahead, who placated the assistants angered by Houdini's outbursts of arrogance, who saw to it—as his mother had had to do—that he had three meals a day no matter how interested he was in practising a new trick, that his suits were pressed and his shirts clean.

But that June day in 1894, Bessie looked just

what she was—the thin, small, naïve daughter of a strict German Catholic widow; a young bride aghast at the strange new world she had inexplicably married into. Apparently there was never any sense of strain between Mrs. Weiss and her son's new wife; Houdini's devotion to his mother had not lessened in the least when he married. And little Gladys, Mrs. Weiss's only daughter, found Bessie a playful and affectionate older sister, a wonderful story-teller, and an understanding friend.

Bessie was very young, however—even younger than her years in some ways—and very easily frightened. And there was much to frighten her. She would have run sobbing to her mother a dozen times during the first weeks, if Mrs. Rahner had been willing to receive her. But her family had refused to accept the marriage, and closed their door to Bessie. She couldn't go home —though she often wanted to.

Her curly-haired young husband, sometimes so gay, could also seem so strange—almost so sinister—that she was terrified. It even occurred to her superstition-filled mind that she had perhaps married a devil. Houdini could work magic, and her credulity about the reality of the magic was even stronger than Houdini's had been on the day he first saw the Great Merlin.

Houdini, a whole year older than Bessie and—

he thought—infinitely wiser, laughed at her fears and slowly taught her to forget them.

"You never told me what your father's name was," he said casually one night, when they were alone in the cheap little furnished room where they had set up housekeeping. "No—don't say it," he hurried on, as Bessie opened her mouth. "Write it down."

Bessie had forgotten, as Houdini was certain she had, that the name had appeared on their marriage license and on the forms they had later filled out when they were remarried by both a Jewish rabbi and a Catholic priest. Meekly she did as he asked.

"Don't let me see it. Now fold it up," Houdini commanded. "And then burn the paper. Here—you can use the gas jet."

Bessie was frightened again. This was more of the mysterious behavior she feared. But Houdini's eyes had an almost hypnotic power. She didn't dare disobey him. The paper was burned.

Carefully Houdini collected the ash and, pushing up his sleeve, rubbed the gray powder into his arm.

Gradually, to Bessie's horrified amazement, her father's name, Gebhart, began to glow through the ash, in letters the color of blood.

Finally Bessie found her voice and her strength, and ran screaming toward the door. When Hou-

dini caught her she struggled wildly to free herself.

"Let me go! Let me go!"

"It was only a trick, you silly," Houdini said.
"Listen to me. I said it was only a trick." And
while she still struggled, he hurried on. "I'll tell
you just how I did it. I knew the name all along,
of course. So I just mixed up some. . . ."

He showed her the ingredients he had used.
With one free hand—and holding her firmly
with the other—he illustrated how the ash had
given color to the letters previously and invisibly
inscribed on his arm.

"You just have to know how to do it," he insisted. "There's nothing to it if you just know
the trick."

At last she had to believe him. He made it all
so clear. And finally, as Houdini initiated her, one
by one, into the mysteries of magic, she gradually
came to share his own curiosity about the tricks
that he and other magic-makers performed.

Even so, she needed a little time to get used to
the idea which, she found, Houdini and all the
Weiss family took for granted: the idea that she
would assume Theo's place in the act. She had
been brought up to believe that the stage was,
in the good old-fashioned phrase, a "den of in-
iquity." The Weiss brothers had, in fact, been
the first performers she had ever seen. But Houdini wanted her help. And Houdini was not, she

had finally decided, a devil after all. The stage had not harmed him. It need not harm her, either. She put on one of Mother Weiss's skirts, in order to feel more grownup, and conscientiously applied herself to learning her new job of wife and assistant.

There was one more shock to survive, when Houdini first showed her the tights she would have to wear for their performance. Bessie rebelled and wept, but again she gave in. And when she put them on, together with the blouse that was startlingly low in the neck—it actually touched her collarbone—she found it wasn't so bad after all. The heavens didn't fall. No avenging power struck her down for her lack of modesty.

Within a few weeks after the marriage the new act was ready. It even received a brief newspaper notice, in the columns of the *Coney Island Clipper*, stating that Harry Houdini had bought out his brother's interest in the Houdini Brothers' act, and that "their mysterious box mystery" would thenceforth be performed by Harry and his wife, the former "Miss Bessie Raymond." When she read the notice Bessie proved she had already acquired enough of the performer's temperament to resent the misspelling of her name.

They were ready to go on. They only needed a chance. But unfortunately the new act had little better luck than the old one. There were, again, occasional beer hall performances, and Houdini resented them particularly now because he felt his wife shouldn't be subjected to the easy, often rude, familiarity of the beer-drinkers. The truth was they paid very little attention to Bessie. She was so small—she weighed only ninety pounds, at a time when a woman's attractiveness was measured largely by her size—that if the patrons noticed her at all they thought of her as "just a kid." Managers sometimes reacted the same way to Bessie's stature, and in their case it was more disastrous. One flatly refused them an audition, the moment he saw Bessie. "What do you think I'm running?" he demanded. "A kindergarten?"

But they found jobs of some sort, here and there, around New York at first, and then drifting farther from home, in the small towns toward the west. When they were close to Chicago, Harry got in touch with a Mr. Hedges, the manager of Kohl and Middleton, who agreed to give the Great Houdinis a spot for a while. But when the Chicago job was over it was the same old story: one-night stands and beer hall dates, in and out of Chicago, in and out of New York, riding on dusty day coaches, and always taking the cheapest lodgings they could find wherever they were.

They kept assuring themselves that one day—and one day very soon—an agent for one of the new vaudeville circuits would see them, and they would be lifted to fame overnight.

The vaudeville circuit, a newcomer to the field of entertainment, had come into being as the result of the success of a few places like Tony Pastor's in New York. At its inception, Pastor's was a novel institution. Its owner, a veteran singer and clown himself, had been suddenly struck with the thought that the beer hall and the music hall, prosperous as they sometimes were, attracted only men. Husbands never considered bringing their wives, nor young men their girls, and the women would have refused such an invitation if it had been given. In the Victorian era respectability was important, and for its strait-laced defenders beer hall entertainment was one of the principal targets.

Tony Pastor decided that, from a purely business point of view, this was unfortunate. Profits could be doubled if women as well as men patronized an establishment. With great care he planned and opened a hall where no smoking or drinking was allowed, where only "clean" entertainment—or "variety," as it was called—was permitted, and he invited the ladies to attend. The venture met with quick and decided public approval. Soon Pastor could afford to move from the small Hoym Theater on New York's Bowery to a larger Broadway house, and to pay such large salaries that every artist in the country stormed his doors. He presented many well-established European performers, and gave the best of the American acts a chance. Many great careers had their start at Pastor's. It was there that the popular Irish Maggie Cline sang, night after night, her famous song, "Throw Him Down, McCloskey." It was there that the beautiful Lillian Russell made her debut with such heart-rending lyrics as "Kiss Me, Mother, Ere I Die."

Other managers, of course, immediately followed Pastor's lead. The hitherto neglected female audience had proved a gold mine. New halls opened everywhere. Soon big business began to take an interest, and wealthy investors bought up whole groups of these halls. Under their management the variety, or vaudeville, circuit was developed: an act would be hired not for one hall, but for several, to be played in turn. And a performer so fortunate as to sign a contract with the Keith or the Proctor management, for example, would thus have work for many weeks, traveling the circuit from one hall to another.

Once the Houdinis came very close to winning one of those wonderful contracts for themselves. E. F. Albee, manager of the Keith circuit and later president of the Keith-Albee theater chain, saw their act one day at Huber's Dime Museum on Fourteenth Street, in New York, and dashed

f to urge his associates to hire the youthful
rformers.

"What are they?" the associates asked. "Did
u say a dime museum act?"

Albee admitted that they were, and his sug-
stion was promptly vetoed. The circuits were
ig time," and the salaries they were able to pay
ve them the pick of the world's artists. And
 those days it was the foreign performers who
ere given preference. Americans still had a spe-
al admiration for everything that was im-
rted, whether it was music, literature, art, fash-
ns, or vaudeville. P. T. Barnum had brought
nny Lind from Europe; it would hardly have
curred to him to go to a great deal of trouble
 publicize a native singer. And, similarly, the
eith management shied away from home-grown
lent, and especially from talent that had here-
fore been recognized only by the shoddy Dime
useum or its counterpart.

But during the winter of 1895 the Houdinis,
aying a round of ill-paying engagements in the
uth, were one day electrified by a telegram.

"Bess!" Harry shouted, staring at the flimsy
llow sheet in his hands.

"What is it?" Bessie was at his side in an in-
nt. He looked as pale as a ghost.

"Oh, nothing, I guess." Houdini attempted a
ile. "It's just a joke, probably. Somebody

thinks it's funny to send us a wire signed Ton
Pastor, and——"

"Tony Pastor!" Bessie snatched the paper awa
from him. The message offered them a spot o
the Pastor bill the following week. "It's not a
joke!" Bessie declared. "How could it be? We
don't know anybody who could afford to throw
money away sending silly telegrams. Oh, Harry
—Tony Pastor wants us! You always knew i
would happen some day. Now it has!"

"Bess, you're right! It has!" Houdini picked
her up and swung her around in their small
shabby room. His moment of doubt was over
fame had reached out and found him, just as he
had always been certain it would.

They had to borrow money from the manager
of the hall they were playing that week in order
to get to New York; they had spent all their savings for ads in the theatrical papers, announcing
"Next week at Tony Pastor's—The Great Houdinis, Harry and Bessie." And the minute they
got off the train they went straight to the theater, to stand proudly in front of the poster which
listed—in the very smallest type, at the very bottom—their own names.

Their pride shriveled a little when they went
inside, and learned that they were to open each
program. This meant that their act would go on
at the worst possible times: in the middle of the
morning, shortly after noon, and at six-thirty in

the evening. Performers appearing at those hours ran little risk of being sighted by scouts for the big circuits or by critics from the theatrical papers. But Tony Pastor had sent for them, and it would be fortune enough if he liked their act.

Tense with nervousness, they gave their first performance—to a handful of disinterested customers and a few bored cleaning women not yet finished with their work. Tony Pastor wasn't present. And he didn't appear for their second show. They knew he was a busy man, but as the hours went by it became more and more difficult to assure each other that things were going well when they had no idea whether they were going at all or not.

"Perhaps," Bessie suggested, "Mr. Pastor doesn't ever bother to watch the show when the star isn't here." They had heard that Maggie Cline, Pastor's headline attraction for that week, was ill at home with a cold.

"Perhaps," Harry agreed glumly.

They were walking toward the wings, ready too early for their evening show, when a warm voice demanded of Bessie, "Who made you up?"

The round red spots of rouge stood out brighter than ever on Bessie's suddenly pale cheeks. It was the great Maggie Cline herself who had stopped them!

"I did," Bessie managed to reply. The next moment she found herself in the star's dressing room, being powdered and primped by expert fingers, and answering a dozen kindly questions about the Great Houdinis and their act.

Bessie was so enchanted at her new image in the mirror—she looked really *old,* she thought admiringly—that she didn't see the big figure who had come to stand in the door. And when Maggie Cline said casually over her shoulder, "Tony, I'm going to watch this kid's act," Bessie had to look twice to assure herself that it was really Tony Pastor there behind her.

"Run along now," Maggie Cline said. "There's your opening music."

Bessie dashed breathlessly out to join Houdini. There wasn't even time to savor the startled admiration on his face.

"They're watching," she breathed. "Maggie Cline and Tony Pastor!"

And then they were on.

They had never given a better performance in their lives. Houdini, confident that for once he was displaying his skill for people who could appreciate it, strutted the stage magnificently. Bessie thought he had never been so splendid. And every time she caught a glimpse of the flower Maggie Cline had pinned to her shoulder, and remembered the way her face had looked when Maggie had added to it the last touch of mascara, she too could move with a new assurance.

Afterward, in their dressing room, they sat

staring at each other. They had done it. They knew they had. Even Tony Pastor must have liked the show they put on that night.

They weren't even surprised when they answered a knock at the door and found him there.

"Well," he said genially, "you kids do a fine act. I'm going to give you a better place tomorrow."

They walked home on air. His words, and Maggie Cline's warm, "Say, you Great Houdinis, you are great," echoed and re-echoed in their ears.

"No more beer halls for us," Houdini said firmly.

"Of course not. Would you rather go out on the Keith circuit or the Proctor, do you think?"

"Oh, I don't know." Houdini waved a casual hand.

But the critics had already looked at Tony Pastor's bill that week—or at most of it, at any rate—and they didn't come back to see the Houdinis when they were moved from first place on the program to the much better fourth. No newspapers proclaimed their greatness. When the week was over, Houdini asked Tony Pastor for an endorsement, and the great man pulled a sheet of paper toward him and wrote, "The Houdinis' act as performed here I found satisfactory and interesting." And that was all there was to it.

They had played at Tony Pastor's, and the world had ignored the event.

They showed Mr. Pastor's statement to a dozen agents, but the agents just nodded and handed it back. After all, it didn't say they were remarkable. "Satisfactory and interesting" was what it said. Plenty of acts were satisfactory. And "interesting"—well, it was a matter of opinion. Audiences didn't seem to care much for that handcuff stuff.

After several grim weeks of discouragement the Houdinis accepted an engagement with Welsh Brothers' Circus. It was a good circus, as circuses went. But Houdini couldn't help but remember that he had played in a circus when he was nine—and that he was now nearly twenty-one. They joined the show at Lancaster, Pennsylvania, at night and in the middle of a driving rain. They were soaked to the skin and splattered with mud by the time they found the tent.

Bessie fell on the cot sobbing, when they had been shown into the tiny curtained-off cubicle that was to be their home in the big traveling car. But Houdini, after the first bad moments, had already begun to work out new routines. He had learned from Mr. Welsh, on their arrival, that Bessie would be expected to do mind-reading and a song-and-dance act; that he himself would work the Punch and Judy show, perform magic, and do his handcuff act; and that together they would do the trunk trick.

"Cheer up, Bess," he said, "we get twenty-five a week and cakes. And——"

"Cakes?" Bessie sobbed.

"Sure. Meals. Come on, now; you'll like it once you get used to it. The folks are all swell, and it's fun riding in the parade. Look, d'you remember the signals for that mind-reading routine we worked out?"

He would have to write some new rhymes for her songs, he was thinking, and brush up on his Punch and Judy techniques. He hadn't done that since his earlier circus days. There was a lot of work to do. It was too bad that fame had postponed its arrival again. But there was no time to worry about it now, and in any case it would come eventually. It had to. It couldn't evade them forever.

6

Even the dime museum schedule had seemed fairly peaceful in comparison with the circus life they now led. They were always pitching the tent or striking it, getting ready for the parade or getting ready for a show, doing one or another of the various acts expected of them. Bessie couldn't understand how Harry could manage, as he regularly did, to spend time every day with an elderly Japanese in the company. The old performer was a "swallower"—he could gulp down whole oranges and bring them up again. Some of Houdini's enthusiasms—this was one of them—made Bessie nervous. She wished Houdini *were* too busy to be so perpetually curious.

But on the whole she soon felt pleasantly at home with the Welsh Brothers' Circus. There was an air of fine camaraderie about the troupe. The other two women performers, both much older than she, were soon treating Bessie like a daughter.

She got special treats from the cook and little presents from everyone. It was a relief not to have to struggle to appear so grownup all the time.

And she and Harry were making several extra dollars a week, in addition to their salary. They had learned earlier how to augment their income by selling "trick" decks of cards that they made out of the used decks Harry collected from beer halls and gambling houses—paying for his booty by a few sleight of hand stunts.

But with the Welsh Brothers there proved to be still other possibilities of earning extra money. Harry and another performer obtained the concession for selling soap and toilet articles at a booth set up among the side shows. The two clowns who had the sheet-music concession paid Bessie two dollars a week for singing the choruses of the songs they offered for sale before each show. And Houdini, wearing a few old sacks, his hair rumpled and his face smeared with dirt, sat daily in a cage and played the part of the Wild Man.

The ringmaster always announced that this violent creature subsisted entirely on tobacco and raw meat—and the whole company was delighted that Harry had accepted the assignment, since he always turned over to his fellow-players all the cigarettes and cigars the audience tossed him in return for ferocious growls of thanks.

Altogether the Houdinis were establishing themselves on a sound financial basis, they thought. They were sending Mrs. Weiss twelve dollars a week, and still managing to put by most of their basic salary. At the end of the circus season their savings were considerable. Harry promptly invested the money in a traveling show called "The American Gaiety Girls."

He had decided that the way to get ahead quickly, to win the respect, as well as the attention, of theater managers, was to have his own company.

"Now we won't have to kowtow to agents any longer," he told Bess grandly. "We'll get our own bookings. We'll play wherever we like."

The truth was, however, that it proved difficult to play anywhere at all. Houdini never had very good judgment in business matters. This early venture was no exception. After the contracts were signed he discovered that he had purchased a half-interest in a sizeable debt, as well as in a weary, discouraged chorus and a handful of battered specialty acts. The show limped painfully from town to town, from bad to worse. Sometimes there was enough money in the till to pay salaries, just as often there was not.

The Houdinis themselves did their best to whip new life into the program. They gave their own numbers, played in the lurid one-act melodrama which was a feature of most shows in those days, and filled in frantically for delinquent members of the company. The night Harry substituted at the last moment for both the singer and the comedian was perhaps the grimmest night of all. He had no voice, and he certainly wasn't funny.

He did for a while, however, confidently believe he could win support for the troupe by obtaining publicity for himself. As soon as they entered a new town he would present himself at the local police headquarters and offer to prove that he could extricate himself from the chief's handcuffs. Sometimes he was sent brusquely about his business; sometimes he was allowed to try the cuffs, and won a reluctant or admiring round of applause for his success. One chill winter day in Holyoke, Massachusetts, he even hit the newspaper with his triumph. In the Holyoke *Daily Democrat* for December 2, 1895, the following story appeared:

HAS NO USE FOR HANDCUFFS

THE POLICE ENTERTAINED BY A STRANGER WHO UNFASTENS ANY PAIR OF HANDCUFFS PUT ON HIM

Harry Houdini of the American Gaiety Girl Company, which plays at the Empire this week, walked into the police station yesterday afternoon to see if the police had any handcuffs which they couldn't manage. Mr. Houdini is an expert in unlocking these instruments and he can manage them as well when they are around his wrists as when fastened to some one else.

"I am traveling with the Gaiety Company," said he to Officer Chamberlain who was seated in the office. "I thought I would drop in and show you a little trick with the handcuffs. Put any sort of cuff around my wrists, lock it and take away the key; let me go into a side room for a second and I will return with the leaders unfastened."

"A rather doubtful statement," thought Officer Chamberlain, but nevertheless he thought he would give the fellow a trial, so he pulled out his own manacles and fastened them around Mr. Houdini's wrists, putting the key in his pocket. Then the fellow walked into an adjoining room and shut the door. In less than a minute he returned carrying the handcuffs in his hand. This astonishing performance was repeated twice with equal success each time.

It makes no difference with Mr. Houdini what kind of handcuffs are produced. He unlocks them all with as much ease as if they were strings wound around his wrists.

Houdini, of course, was delighted. Thereafter he never failed to visit police stations to make the same offer, though it didn't always result in similar publicity. But since his show was, by then, playing only in the smallest towns, and the newspapers were equally small, even the occasional notices he received stirred no echoes in the cosmopolitan world; in fact, they had little publicity value even in the towns where he appeared. The American Gaiety Girls seemed beyond hope. Houdini finally abandoned his managerial career a good deal poorer than when he had taken it on.

But before long he was involved in another business venture.

It began auspiciously enough as a better-than-usual engagement. They were hired to join the show organized by a man who called himself Marco—a gentle, kindly person with as little financial acumen as Houdini himself. Marco, by profession a church organist, by avocation a magician, had satisfied the ambition of a lifetime by getting together his troupe and setting out with it on a tour that began in Nova Scotia. He admired the Houdinis' work, especially the handcuff act—which in Houdini's eyes marked him as a man of true discernment—and introduced them proudly as one of his top specialty numbers. But for one reason or another the show failed from the start. Even before the Nova Scotia engagements were fulfilled, the original company had been reduced to Marco, a stage manager, and the Great Houdinis. Marco accepted defeat and returned home, leaving his equipment in Houdini's hands.

Harry and Bessie tried desperately to salvage something from the wreckage. Grimly they played a series of drafty schoolhouses, dreary beer halls, and whatever other halls would permit them the use of a stage for the night. Houdini finally admitted he was discouraged—although not about his profession, of course. No matter how dire their straits, he always felt that it was only the present situation that had failed them, never the world of magic itself. He never grew so depressed that he couldn't lose himself in the thought of a new idea for perfecting his act.

And now, in the town of St. John, New Brunswick, he visited an insane asylum and became fascinated by the sight of one of the more violent inmates struggling in the confines of a strait jacket. Harry immediately forgot his managerial troubles, borrowed the jacket for the duration of his stay, and took it back to his room. He had realized that the ability to dislocate the shoulders —and Harry could dislocate one of his—would have enabled the prisoner to obtain some slack in the stiff material, and thus free his arms. At the end of a week's daily practice Houdini had learned how to twist and contort his body in such a way that he could actually free himself from the restraining garment.

Immediately he was the showman again. He offered the feat that very night on the stage, convinced that it would win him the acclaim he felt he deserved. Volunteers were invited to fasten him into the strait jacket. He then disappeared behind a curtain and some time later—much dishevelled, exhausted, and aching—he reappeared free. There was scarcely a ripple of applause. The audience took for granted he had been faking— that his worn appearance had been deliberately contrived in an effort to persuade them that he had actually suffered the tortures it suggested.

The strait jacket release was eventually to be among Houdini's most spectacularly successful stunts. But he had not yet learned how to present it in an effective manner, how to win recognition for the skill, strength, and agility it demanded.

The strait jacket release did not, therefore, revitalize the faltering remains of the Marco show. By the time Harry, too, admitted its end, there was not even enough money in his pockets for fare home. He and Bessie slept in a doorway one night, and the next morning she set off to try to persuade the captain of a southbound passenger ship to take them along as free guests. They would, she explained, pay for their passage with a performance. It was one of the many occasions when Bessie's size and her generally fragile and wistful appearance won the day. The captain agreed.

Lightheaded with hunger they mounted the gangplank, promising each other that they would give the best show of their lives. But two minutes later Houdini was prostrate on his berth, desperately seasick. Bessie, convinced that he would recover shortly, lugged their heavy paraphernalia to the lounge and set everything up in readiness. Hours went by. Houdini was worse rather than better. Finally, her hands shaking, Bessie attempted the routine herself. A sympathetic member of the audience cut short the pitiful recital by rising to pass the hat for contributions. Bessie's "take" was twenty-five dollars, and she was convinced that their luck had turned.

But Houdini's jaundiced view of the world that day proved more accurate than hers. They had some of the worst jobs of their career during the next months, and some of the longest stretches of being entirely without work. They tried anything and everything, so long as it was within the realm of "the profession."

One minor, but fairly steady, source of funds was Harry's sale, on a commission basis, of magical equipment furnished by Gus Roteberg, of Chicago, one of the country's leading suppliers of magic goods. Houdini's attempt to inaugurate a correspondence school of magic was less remunerative. When a long period of reverses drove him one day to offer to sell his own handcuff secrets to each of six New York newspapers, he was unable to find a buyer for his most cherished possession.

In those discouraging years—1896, 1897, 1898 —it seemed as if the Houdinis were truly doomed to perpetual failure. They changed the name of their act to "Harry Houdini" when Bessie pointed out that she had never heard of a husband-and-wife team that was truly successful on the stage; but even this generous gesture proved fruitless.

The Kohl and Middleton Dime Museum still took them on at irregular intervals, but most of the intervening jobs they had were of short life and abrupt termination. Sometimes it seemed as if the Houdinis had only to join a company for it to fail, leaving them stranded in some strange town utterly without friends or funds.

Houdini made his own sacrifice too: he discarded the handcuff release from their act, convinced at long last that it was something in which an audience could never become interested. In its place he presented himself as "Houdini, the King of Cards." He could scale a card into the air in such a way that it would travel away from him in a wide arc—and then return to his hands. And he could make cards disappear with a wave of his hand, and reappear again as quickly. He did conjuring, too. He produced live pigeons and guinea pigs out of a silk hat. He borrowed a watch, smashed it—or so it seemed to the alarmed owner —rammed the broken bits into a gun, fired them at a target poised on Bessie's head, and the watch appeared miraculously whole again. He did magic "dyeing" too, thrusting white handkerchiefs, one by one, through a simple paper tube, and pulling them out at the other end, each "dyed" a different color.

"Anthro-pro-po-lay-gos," Houdini would intone slowly, as he pushed each white square out of sight. It was his own special "magic" phrase, utterly without meaning, but apparently, in his own ears at least, of profoundly mysterious significance.

The Great Trunk Mystery, however, was stil
their best trick, and Bessie had long ago learned
her role in it to perfection. Their equipment
would be inspected by a committee from the
audience; Harry's hands would then be tied behind his back; he would be lifted into a large sack
the mouth of which would be drawn together,
knotted, and sealed over his head; and the sack
would be put into the trunk which in turn would
be locked, roped, and sealed.

The committee would stand aside at that moment, and Bessie would take her place between
the curtains, holding one in each hand. "Ladies
and gentlemen," she would say, spacing the words
clearly and distinctly as Houdini had rehearsed
her, "you see the locked and roped trunk into
which Houdini has been placed, with his wrists
securely bound behind his back, his entire body
sealed within the sack, and the sack locked within
the trunk—he on the inside, I on the outside."
Slowly she would begin to draw the curtains together. "I shall clap my hands three times—and
you watch for the effect."

One—two—three! She brought her small hands
together in sharp claps, and immediately after the
third one, she drew the curtains closed in front of
herself with a flourish. Almost instantly they
were flung wide again, and Houdini would be
bowing to the audience, his hands free, the coat
of his dress suit mysteriously missing. Bessie would

of course thereafter be discovered inside the bag, inside the trunk, her hands bound by the original tapes—and wearing Houdini's coat.

Nobody ever examined the bag and noticed that it had been slit open at the bottom; nobody ever found the concealed escape panel in the trunk. The speed with which the Houdinis performed, made the transformation appear truly unbelievable and beyond explanation.

But when the Great Trunk Mystery no longer won them billings, when they could not sell the dreadful act of "comedy and pathos" which they worked up especially for the beer hall audience—offering Bessie as a small girl, wearing a dress made out of her best nightgown, and Harry as a down-and-out tramp singing tearfully of the little daughter he had lost—when even this compromise with their ideals had failed to earn them steady work, the Houdinis turned to a type of performance almost certain to be sure-fire in those days. They weren't particularly proud of the move, but neither were they seriously disturbed. They had a living to make, and this was merely one way to do it. Harry and Bessie became "spiritualists."

7

Much later in his life, when Houdini was an active and vociferously articulate campaigner against fraudulent "mediums," he was embarrassed to recall that in his own early days he had practised mediumship himself—and of a deliberately fraudulent kind. At the time, of course, he felt that hunger justified this expedient. He was also inclined to feel that his credulous clients got no more than they deserved: they were so foolish as to scorn Houdini the magician, and yet be willing to pay Houdini the medium for whatever "information" he chose to offer. He had little compunction about collecting his data from local graveyards, from the medium's "bluebook" giving pertinent facts about ardent believers in various communities, or by posing as a traveling salesman and stealing glances at the family Bible while a housewife examined his wares. And of course he made good use of the book he and Joe

Rinn had studied so carefully in the old Pastime A. C. days.

Harry and Bessie had for some time been fairly adept at a mind-reading turn, and this made a good basis for their "séance." Bessie, blindfolded and in a convincingly "trancelike" state, was able to repeat whatever facts Houdini secretly conveyed to her about various persons present—that, for example, Mrs. M. was a widow and would be eagerly awaiting a message that her late husband was well and happy in "the beyond," or that Mr. J. had recently buried his daughter and sought reassurance as to the girl's bliss in heaven.

Houdini's own specialty was one which the Davenport Brothers, famous early spiritualists, had made known all over the world, to the confusion and controversy of experts who argued then —as they still argue today—whether spirits can and do communicate with the living. Houdini followed the Davenports' pattern faithfully in his performance. To assure his audience that he could have no part in the bell ringing, the "voices," and the other manifestations they were about to experience, he would allow himself to be roped and tied and locked into a cabinet. The lights would then be completely extinguished, and the expected events would occur: the bell would ring, the "voices" speak, the ominous thumps and knocks would be heard. When the lights were turned on again, Houdini would be found still secure in his bonds. His audience never seemed to suspect that it was child's play for the conjurer to extricate himself long enough to produce the phenomena, and then slip back into his restraints before the lights exposed him.

They gave a séance in St. Joseph, Missouri, one evening for the usual reason: they were broke. They had already spent two weeks in the town, doing the trunk trick and Houdini's card manipulations at "The Eden Musée, or Wonderland." Its owner had been unable to meet any salaries the first week, and had thereupon permitted the performers to stay on for a second under their own management—that is, they were allowed the use of the hall, and could keep all proceeds for themselves. Over all the Eden's posters the performers had pasted streamers announcing the fact that they were being held over "by popular demand," but nobody had been fooled. Their audiences continued small and unenthusiastic, except for one magic-struck high-school student who attended almost every performance, planting himself devotedly before Houdini's platform.

Houdini recognized him. When he and Bess had played St. Joe's the previous year, young Ralph Read had introduced himself and confided that he, too, hoped to be a magician some day. Harry had taught the youngster a few card tricks, encouraged his interest in magic, and won himself a staunch admirer.

84

Now, as he and Bessie sat glumly in the lobby of the Commercial Hotel at the end of their second fatal week, still unable to pay their way out of town, but equally unable to remain longer as the Commercial's guests, at the rate of a dollar a day for room and board, they saw young Ralph in the street and called him in.

"Tell me, Read," Houdini said, "do you think a spirit show would go well here?"

Flattered at having his advice sought, Ralph assured him that St. Joe was enthusiastic about such things, that it had, in fact, a large number of earnest believers.

Together they planned the performance. Ralph's knowledge of the town was invaluable. With his aid—and on his guarantee—a hall was secured, announcements printed on credit, and the event scheduled for Sunday evening. They were talking over their final plans, when Ralph said eagerly, "Suppose I bring along a pair of handcuffs. Wouldn't it be a good stunt if you were manacled as well as tied up inside the cabinet?"

Houdini glanced at Bessie, hardly able to believe that someone was suggesting he perform a handcuff release. Of course the suggestion was coming from a boy who didn't know Houdini as the Handcuff King; Read intended the release itself to be no part of the visible act. But even so

85

Houdini couldn't help but feel that it was a hopeful sign.

"Bess," he said, with a wink, "the boy wants to bring handcuffs to the séance."

"Well, wouldn't it be all right?" Read went on. "It would look good for you to be handcuffed in the cabinet. Nobody would believe you could do anything tricky then."

"Bess," Houdini eyed her again, "the boy thinks it would look good for me to be handcuffed inside the cabinet." He turned back to Read. "Where would you get the handcuffs?"

"I've got three pair. My uncle gave them to me. They used to belong to the police department. I'll tell you what kind they are, and then you'll know which one you want me to bring. They—"

Houdini stopped him with a quickly raised hand. "No. Don't tell me anything about the cuffs. Don't tell me who made them, or what they look like. I want to be able to say that I have never seen nor touched the cuffs in my life. Just bring one pair, whichever one you like, and the key that fits it. When you come up on the stage with them you will lock them on some member of the audience first, and keep the key; the audience will see then that it's impossible for the fellow to escape. After that you'll lock them on *me* and put the key in your pocket. You'll keep it there throughout the whole show—understand?"

"Yes, sir." Read was enormously impressed, but

he was a magician himself, and he yearned for Houdini's approval. "And there's something else. I can tell you a secret about these cuffs—how you can get them open even when the keyhole has been sealed. Then you could——"

Houdini stopped him again. "Don't tell me anything. Yes, of course you must seal the keyhole when you fasten them on me. Seal it well." His rare smile flashed out. "But don't worry about my producing spirit manifestations. There'll be plenty doing inside that cabinet, no matter how securely I've been manacled."

There was a good crowd on hand Sunday night. Ralph had told everybody in town

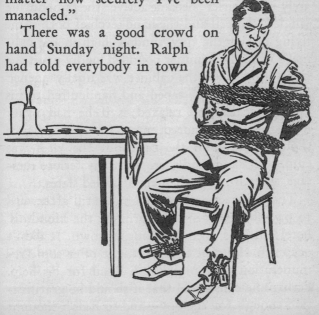

that the Great Houdini was to give a séance. Most of the audience consisted of genuine believers, and some of them were disappointed—Houdini produced no voices to answer their questions. But the handcuff addition was effective. The cuffs were locked on Houdini after he was sitting in the cabinet, one half of the pair fastened to his chair, the other half to his already-bound hands. A tambourine, a bell, a slate, a glass of water, and a handkerchief were placed on the table beside him, and the cabinet was closed. Almost immediately the "spirits" became active: the tambourine jangled, the bell and the handkerchief both came flying out of the tiny window high in the cabinet's wall, the hammer pounded loudly upon the table. And when the cabinet was finally opened again, Houdini sat, taped and handcuffed to his chair, as calm and relaxed as if he had never moved—which, indeed, most of the audience thought had been the case. But the glass was empty of water, and there was a mysterious message written inside the pair of sealed slates.

There was enough money in the till afterward to pay the hall rent, the printer, the Houdinis' hotel bill, and their fare out of town. It didn't occur to Houdini that he might offer some remuneration to young Ralph Read for his help. Perhaps he considered that it should be gratification enough for the boy—and so Ralph thought it was—to have aided so gifted a performer as himself.

A year later Houdini was back in St. Joseph, still presenting his magic and "Metamorphosis," the trunk trick. (On that visit he permitted young Read to bring him some used decks of cards, from which he made the trick decks he sold from the platform.) But his hope in the handcuff release was still high. He had pretty well given up his spiritualistic act by then—a few rather startling events had occurred which made both him and Bessie wary of remaining intimate with the "spirits."

Once Harry had predicted that the son of one of his clients would fall from his bicycle and break his arm. Houdini had seen the boy and his bicycle outside the window and spoke—so he always insisted—purely at random, out of the necessity to predict something for the woman's satisfaction. But the minor tragedy took place shortly after he had foretold it, and it frightened him to be hailed as a true clairvoyant.

On another occasion, in a small Canadian town, Bessie answered the query of a Mary Murphy, who had for years been searching for her brother, by assuring the woman that he would be found at a specific address in New York City. There was indeed a Murphy at that address. He owned an ice-cream store near the Weiss home, and he had popped into Bessie's mind the moment the name was mentioned. But she was as amazed as her client—and alarmed rather than pleased—when the New York Murphy proved to be the one Mary Murphy had been seeking for years. The Houdinis were extremely relieved when a few other jobs began coming their way, and they could leave the "spirits" to other "mediums."

They even preferred to work briefly in a company that presented ancient, time-worn melodramas—such as "Ten Nights in a Barroom." During this period Harry used an assumed name in order to preserve "Houdini" for what he persistently regarded as his true profession. When they were with the Welsh Brothers Circus again in the spring of 1898, he wrote in his new diary that he was thinking of relearning the acrobatics that had earned him his first job: acrobats seemed currently in greater demand than magicians.

He changed his mind about that. But at the end of that year something happened which did convince him, for the first and only time, that he ought to give up his dream forever and accept the offer Bessie's brother-in-law had made to obtain work for him in a lock factory.

8

"But Harry, you'd be miserable in a lock factory," Bessie pointed out for the hundredth time, as they hurried along the street toward Kohl and Middleton's Dime Museum, where they were playing at the time.

"Naturally I would. But do you think I'm happy now?"

The argument had been going on since the night before, when Harry had met what seemed to him the most catastrophic blow in his career.

He had been billed once more at the Dime Museum as a handcuff artist, and the previous evening a Chicago detective in the audience had, with Houdini's permission, locked him into a pair of cuffs which he was challenged to open. Houdini had accepted with perfect assurance, chiefly interested in the flurry of curiosity aroused in the crowd. The cuffs looked ordinary enough. He expected to be out of them in an instant.

But minutes went by—long agonizing minutes —and he had not succeeded. The audience around his platform grew restive, jeered at him finally, and then drifted away. At the end of a tortured hour he was still shackled, and entirely alone in the hall except for the grimly amused detective at his side.

"I might as well tell you," the detective said at last, "that cuff don't open. I fixed a slug in it, and it won't unlock."

Houdini's head snapped up, furious anger blazing in his eyes. His forehead was running with sweat, his arms and body aching. But all he could think of was that his professional career was ruined; the audience that had walked out on him that night would never return to hear the explanation of his failure; Mr. Hedges, the manager, would probably fire him on the spot and— with justification, Harry thought—circulate word of his defeat so thoroughly that no one else would ever hire him again.

"So it's no use, Bess," he repeated as they reached Kohl and Middleton's that morning. "I don't even want to go in. They'll laugh at me, and I—"

He didn't have to finish the sentence. Bessie

knew as well as he did that being laughed at was the one thing Houdini could never face.

But she pulled him stubbornly up the steps and thrust the door open. Mr. Hedges was standing just inside, his watch in his hand, his face suffused with fury.

"Do you realize you're late again?" he demanded. "Get out there on the platform. I'm not running a rest cure here, you know."

Hedges was postponing his more serious accusation, Houdini thought as they hurried numbly to their dressing room. He wished he'd forced the matter into the open then and there, so it would be over and done with.

Throughout the morning he waited, tense, to answer with his fist the first grin that greeted him from one of the other performers. But no sign came; they, too, were teasing him, he thought. And when Mr. Hedges strolled through the Hall of Freaks and Miracle Workers sometime later, merely smiled vaguely at the Houdinis and passed on, Houdini was more depressed than ever.

Finally he could endure the suspense no longer and sought Mr. Hedges out between shows. "Well," he said, "what are they saying about me, after last night?"

"After last night?" Hedges looked maddeningly blank.

"When I couldn't get out of the cuff. It had been fixed, of course, but I——"

"Oh! Didn't you ever get out of that thing? This is the first I'd heard about it. Cuff was fixed, you say? Well, what's the difference?"

Houdini went slowly back to his platform, his eyes glazed with misery. The defeat of the Handcuff King had been a bitter enough pill to swallow. That the defeat had gone entirely unnoticed was far worse. It was all Bessie could do, that night, to persuade Harry not to write a letter accepting that factory job immediately.

But gradually a plan that would win him justification began to take shape in his mind. He would make the entire police force of Chicago admit his ability. He would go to the huge city jail—But no, he wouldn't just casually walk in and suggest a test, as he had done in so many other towns. This time he would arrange matters in such a way that his success—and he was determined to be successful—would be publicly acknowledged.

He began his campaign by scraping acquaintance with several newspaper reporters. Then, with a formal introduction, he went with Bessie to call on Andy Rohan, lieutenant of detectives, a close associate of the chief of police. Bessie had her instructions. She was to entertain the big redmustached lieutenant and thus distract his attention, while Houdini made a careful examination of the city jail's lock system. Houdini's experience at Kohl and Middleton's had taught him one lesson he was never to forget: always to examine ahead of time whatever lock he was to attempt.

Their visit was only a partial success. Lieutenant Rohan was entertained, but Houdini found the locks too complicated to yield their secrets to a single brief examination. The next day they repeated their call. Bessie was nervous. This time, she felt, their unexplained sociability might seem odd. And she was right. Rohan, suddenly suspicious, cut the visit short. The hospitality of the city jail, he made clear, was only for those who had business there.

But Houdini had already managed to discover how the locks worked. He left without argument. Then he looked up his newspaper friends and told them that if he were to be handcuffed and locked in a cell of their city jail, he would be able to escape.

Their local pride was aroused. They doubted his claim, of course, but they were curious enough to agree to watch the experiment. Picking up a photographer on the way, they all went to Rohan's office.

"I, Harry Houdini, challenge you to shackle and imprison me in such a way that I cannot release myself."

The announcement brought Rohan swinging around in his chair. "Oh, you do, do you?" The big face was as red as its mustache. But the flaring anger was brought under control as the lieutenant noticed the reporters ranged behind Houdini; publicity was as pleasant to Rohan as it was to a performer.

A moment later he had blandly agreed to the test, certain that he could give the brash husband of that nice little Mrs. Houdini the defeat he deserved.

Houdini was handcuffed and locked into a cell. And he emerged a few moments later, free.

But he discovered that his well-laid plan had gone awry. The reporters were angry rather than impressed.

"What do you take us for, Houdini?" one demanded. "You've spent plenty of time around here before today—Rohan's just told us. There's no trick to taking a wax impression of those locks. You can't play us for fools, you know."

"I'm sorry," Houdini said quickly. "I should have asked you to search me first. Search me now and then lock me up again. Perhaps then you'll believe I don't have any keys in my pocket."

After a moment's indecision they decided to give him another chance. His clothes were removed and locked into another cell, his mouth—at Houdini's own suggestion—was sealed shut, and he was thoroughly searched. Naked except for the handcuffs on his wrists, Houdini was locked into his cell again.

When he reappeared within a few minutes, fully clothed, their amazement was obvious enough to satisfy even Houdini. Rohan's open-mouthed astonishment afforded him particular pleasure.

The next day's papers carried the story of Houdini's success, *and* Houdini's picture.

"Bess! I'm famous!" Houdini shouted, thrusting the still damp sheet under her nose.

Then he dashed back into the street to spend all their available funds for stamps and envelopes, and for more copies of the flattering notice. And they spent the rest of the day clipping, folding, and mailing the evidence of his triumph.

The memory of the detective who had plugged that cuff at the Dime Museum had been gloriously avenged.

Chicago's recognition was the first of what proved to be a series of similar big-city reactions. Houdini felt as if he had at long last manufactured the lockpick he had needed—the one that would open the way to public acclaim: "I, Harry Houdini, challenge. . . ."

In San Francisco he was stripped, locked in a cell, his arms burdened with four pairs of handcuffs, his legs shackled, and one of them inserted in an Oregon boot—a contraption weighing fifty-five pounds and sealed with a combination lock. When he freed himself that time, the chief of police gave his endorsement of the fact, and then issued a statement that was a curiously back-handed compliment.

"Should Houdini turn out to be a criminal," he declared, "I would consider him a very dangerous man, and I suggest that the various officers throughout the United States remember his appearance in case of future emergency."

Houdini smiled to himself. The chief had expressed his own desires exactly; he, too, was determined that the "various officers throughout the United States"—and a good many other people besides—should "remember his appearance."

However, except for a single engagement at Chicago's Hopkins Theater—a quick but brief burst of good fortune resulting directly from that first story—the Houdinis went on playing the dime museums. But Houdini was no longer discouraged. His scrapbook was swelling daily. Soon, he thought—perhaps the very next time they played a city where one of the big circuits had a headquarters—he would walk boldly into its office and demand an audition. Surely no one could fail to be impressed by notices like these, and by the endorsements of the police in a dozen big cities.

They were in Milwaukee the night a stranger invited them to have a cup of coffee with him after the show. He seemed pleasant and intelligent. Houdini agreed, and opened their conversation at the restaurant table with the performer's inevitable first question.

"What did you think of our act?"

"I think you're a rotten showman," the stranger replied.

Houdini stared at him, and the hand holding his coffee cup lowered itself slowly to the table.

"Why don't you cut out the little magical stuff?" the stranger went on, unperturbed. "It only distracts the audience. Why not just give a couple of the big thrillers—like the handcuffs and the trunk trick?"

Houdini was still too startled to answer or to get up and walk out on this impertinent meddler.

"There are plenty of magicians doing the stock stuff," the quiet voice went on, "and doing it very well, at forty per. You have two big stunts at which nobody else can touch you. I'll try you out on the circuit at sixty dollars, and if you make it go, I'll raise you."

Then at long last he told them his name. "I'm Martin Beck," the stranger said.

Houdini's cup rattled noisily against the saucer, and Bess gasped. Martin Beck represented the Orpheum circuit.

"Well—" Houdini cleared his throat—"I think we'll accept your offer, Mr. Beck."

"Good." Martin Beck smiled. "I'll bill you for the summer season. You'll open in June, in San Francisco."

The Houdinis had at last hit the big time.

They finished their spring engagements in a glow of dazzled anticipation. Then they reorganized their act, abandoning with a good deal of sentimental remorse the pretty white pigeons and the plump little guinea pigs that had been their pets and stage properties for so long. Houdini would have liked to think of himself as the complete all-round magician—outstanding at conjuring, at card manipulations, at escapes. But he saw quite clearly, though he hadn't been able to reason it out for himself, that Martin Beck was right when he recommended the presentation of only a few effects. That, Houdini saw now, was showmanship: it was the equivalent of aiming at a target with one or two sizeable bullets, instead of spattering the entire vicinity with buckshot. He had Martin Beck to thank for more than a contract.

There were moments before their opening when Bessie, at least, forgot how grateful she was to the Orpheum representative. While Harry and she were crowded together into a lower berth during the long trip west; while they made their meals frugally out of food they had packed to take along, only to have the food all spoil by the third day out; when they found their San Francisco hotel alive with fleas, and were rocked in the middle of the night by an earthquake—then even the old beer halls seemed hardly less grim to Bessie than a big-time circuit. But on the very day after their arrival Houdini made a highly successful appearance at the local police station, where he freed himself from a dozen heavy fetters, and then from a leather belt-jacket used in the county asylum. The papers ran the story. Their first bows on the Orpheum stage were greeted with applause from an audience already eager to admire this curly-haired young man. Bessie began to feel better.

Soon they were earning ninety dollars a week, as Martin Beck had promised. Their notices became steadily more enthusiastic; their progress from city to city throughout the West, Middle West, and South brought them a mounting elation. Now Houdini could look back to that evening in Milwaukee when he was nine, and know that the applause for Dr. Lynn had been no more clamorous than his own was now.

His manner on the stage was still intense almost to the point of severity. Showmanship, in his case, never included winning a public's affection. But now that he had discarded the "little magic," now that he was performing only the "big tricks," his sternly formal air seemed better suited to his act. It was no clown who extricated himself from those heavy manacles; it was a man whose serious concentration suggested that his feat was indeed one of incredible difficulty—a feat which could only be performed by an artist of rare and unusual abilities. And Houdini never had to act the role of the artist; it was as natural to him as his own faith in his destiny.

"I, Harry Houdini, challenge. . . ." Wherever they played, the police chief heard those words. Some chiefs jumped at the opportunity to try to defeat this assured young man; others shied away from the possibly adverse publicity if they should fail, but were unable to refuse his challenge because refusal in itself would have been an admission of weakness. Houdini freed himself from all the bonds they could devise—in Los Angeles and Nashville, in Memphis and Kansas City, and in dozens of smaller towns which were nevertheless proud of their modern police equipment.

Within a matter of weeks he began to feel that the ninety dollars, which had looked so handsome when he first received it, was hardly sufficient recompense for a Houdini. Crowds always jammed the theaters where he played; they were—they must be—coming to see him. Finally, half confident, half startled at his own temerity, he asked Beck to raise their salary to a hundred and fifty dollars a week. And Beck agreed.

They celebrated extravagantly. Bessie acquired a fur neckpiece. They mailed handsome presents home to the family. And when someone mispronounced their name—a confused public attempted it variously as How-dinnie, Hoo-dinnie, How-deenie—he corrected the offender with some arrogance. Houdini, pronounced Hoo-dee-nee, was, his tone implied, a name that ought to be known to pretty much everyone in the United States.

He was so sure of their widespread renown that, in the fall when their Orpheum tour was over, they held themselves in readiness to accept whatever best circuit offer they next received. But not even a single such contract was offered. The Houdinis presented, in the phrase of the trade, a "novelty act," and it would not have been considered good business to send them again into the territory they had just covered. The eastern circuits in the big eastern cities—New York, Boston, and Philadelphia—had not yet been made aware of the Handcuff King's triumphs, and therefore did not rush to seek him out.

Baffled, chagrined, more amazed at being dropped from their pinnacle than they had been when they were suddenly raised to it, the Houdinis glumly accepted whatever short-term engagements came their way. The year of 1899 dragged to a dismal close. Sometimes Bessie felt that their success had only been achieved in a dream, so distant and improbable did that brilliant summer already seem.

"We're going to Europe, Bess," Houdini said to her abruptly one day.

Bess stared. And then she jumped up and hugged him ecstatically. "To Europe! How did you manage to get such bookings for us? Harry, you're wonderful!"

"There aren't any bookings." Firmly Houdini put down her arms. "I merely said we were going."

Bessie backed away, puzzled.

"We'll get the bookings when we get there," he said with a flash of the arrogance that always showed when he was crossed. "All the big circuits here grab imported talent. Well, we'll *be* imported—once we've made a big success over there. Then they'll be willing to hire us, all right. You wait and see."

Bessie no longer looked uncertain. Houdini had convinced her, as he usually did.

"Of course they'll hire us then," she said. "It's a wonderful idea! Lots of American performers have done it—T. Nelson Downs, the Koin King, and—well, I'm sure there must be others. When do we leave, Harry? Should I begin to pack?"

They left as soon as they had saved up enough money for a second-class passage. It was late in the spring of 1900, and Houdini was twenty-six years old. Once more he was setting out to conquer the world.

9

But the bravado with which Houdini said good-bye to his family and mounted the gangplank fled completely the instant he entered his cabin below decks. Bravado is no match for seasickness. The voyage was a procession of tortured days and delirium-filled nights. By the time the ship docked in England, Harry was a shrunken, haggard invalid, and Bessie was exhausted too from her long vigil of nursing.

Houdini's remarkable vitality, however, almost immediately reasserted itself once they were on land. His starved body was clamoring for food, and he ate prodigiously while Bessie slept away her weariness in the obscure theatrical boarding-

house where they had found a room. Within a few days they were ready to seize the British lion by its tail. Houdini had his scrapbook under his arm, a list of the principal vaudeville agents in his pocket, and high hope in his heart.

When they returned to their room that night, they were more puzzled than discouraged. For some reason they had been abruptly dismissed each time they were fairly underway with a description of their act. The moment Houdini had begun to quote the notices which described his escapes as "marvelous," his ability as "apparently superhuman," the agent had made it clear that he had no interest in the Houdinis whatsoever.

Their next day's rounds had the same result, and so did those of the following day and the day after that. Bessie found herself counting over their dwindling funds each evening, and beginning to wonder a little desperately how long they could hold out. It was true that there were other Handcuff Kings playing in Britain at the time— there was the Great Cirnoc, for one—but why wouldn't someone give Harry a chance to show that he was the greatest of them all? It was true that the Houdinis came from a land which many British still thought of as woolly and untamed— but wasn't there just one agent, somewhere, who would permit them to demonstrate their skill?

Day after day they walked the crooked streets of London's theatrical district; into one agent's office and out almost as quickly; into another, only to retreat again. Bessie was finding it a little difficult to maintain the air of carefree gaiety which should be the player's hallmark, but each rebuff seemed to make Houdini even more cock-sure for his next interview. They marched into an office one morning, when the money in their pockets had been reduced to an alarmingly small amount, and Harry rushed into his "spiel" despite the feeble protests of the young man behind the desk.

"I say, you know," the young man murmured hastily when Houdini paused to spread open his book of clippings, "I'm not the chap you want to see. He's not here at present. I'm—well, I'm just learning the business, as it were."

"Oh?" Houdini looked at him. They were near-ly of an age, but Houdini with his years of barn-storming behind him felt infinitely more experi-enced. "Well, take a look at these then," he went on, with a smile. "You're not likely to see such notices very often."

The young man glanced down at the book, at the bold black headlines so much more dramatic than the neat typescript of a British paper.

"I say," he murmured again, "you must really be rather good."

"I am," Houdini said simply.

"He's wonderful!" Bessie declared.

The young people exchanged swift involuntary smiles. Bessie was radiant: it had been so long since anyone had treated them with the cordiality and interest this young man was showing. Of course it would probably all come to nothing. If he were just learning the business, he—

"That's my name too, you know," the young man said. "Harry, I mean. Harry Day, it is."

After that things seemed to happen with a rush.

"Look here," Harry Day said, "I'm going to call Slater, the manager of the Alhambra, and ask him to give you a try-out. I—wait here, will you?"

Perhaps Harry Day was something of a magician too. Because within a few minutes he was hurrying the Houdinis along to one of London's finest theaters, and introducing them to C. Dundas Slater.

But Slater was not so easily impressed as Harry Day had been. He had seen thousands of vaudeville acts in his time, and it took a good deal to rouse him. He conceded that "Metamorphosis, The Great Trunk Mystery," was an interesting effect; he dismissed with a wave of his hand the sleights and card tricks Houdini ran through to indicate his versatility; and he admitted that Houdini handled the handcuff release with authority. But when Houdini attempted to emphasize his skill with the cuffs by showing Slater the clippings that referred to Houdini as "a marvel," the manager closed his eyes wearily.

"We've had enough marvels hereabouts," he said. "Mind you, I won't say all turnkeys in the States can be bribed, or that you don't have decent cuffs or decent locks on your jails over there. But I'm afraid I wouldn't be interested in another Handcuff King unless he could open the cuffs at Scotland Yard." And Slater turned away with a gesture of dismissal.

Harry Day looked depressed. But Harry Houdini smiled.

"Can you go with me to the Yard now?" he demanded.

Slater swung around again, startled out of his managerial calm. Houdini was looking straight into his eyes.

"Yes," Slater said slowly. "Yes, I could do that."

Houdini was the calmest passenger in the carriage as they rattled across the London cobblestones. And it was Houdini who answered the curt statement of Mr. Melville, superintendent of the famous police force, once they were inside the big grim building.

Melville had addressed himself to Slater, and with barely concealed impatience. "Our handcuffs aren't made for variety acts," he said. "They *hold*."

"Maybe," Houdini said—and his brashness

The cuffs were snapped around his wrists, and locked down hard.

made Harry Day shiver. "But I still want to try them."

Melville shrugged—but Slater was a prominent man in the British capital. So the superintendent opened a drawer and took out a pair of glittering new bracelets connected by heavy metal links.

"May I see them?" Houdini asked politely.

Melville handed them over without comment; Houdini studied them for a moment and then handed them back.

"Still want to try them?" Melville's tone made it clear that he expected a negative answer.

"Sure."

Slater didn't speak. This young American might not be the greatest handcuff expert in the world, he was thinking, but he certainly had the most confidence.

"All right." Melville rose brusquely to his feet, eager to conclude this farcical interview. "Put your arms around that pillar." And when Houdini had obeyed, the cuffs were snapped around his wrists, and locked down hard. "That's how we fasten Yankee criminals who come over here and get into trouble," Melville said, stepping back. He motioned to Slater, and they moved toward the door. Melville glanced back at the cocky young American securely locked to the pillar his arms embraced. "We'll come back for you in a couple of hours," he said.

"Wait." Houdini spoke before they had taken

half a dozen steps. "I'll go with you." And as he stepped away from the pillar the cuffs fell to the floor with a metallic clatter.

Melville's jaw sagged.

Slater stared for an instant, and then smiled for the first time since the Houdinis had walked into his office.

"Come on back to the theater with me," he said, "and we'll sign a contract right now for a two-week turn."

The press releases were sent out, the handbills printed. THE GREAT HOUDINI, they announced; THE HANDCUFF KING. Slater arranged a special performance for the press, to take place before the night of Houdini's opening.

The special performance was not so much a publicity gesture as it was a gesture of self-protection on Slater's part. During the preparations for it Houdini finally learned the reason for his failure to impress British agents other than the inexperienced Harry Day: the very word "marvel" which Houdini had tossed about so fluently had come to have a frightening sound to theater managers. Two widely-publicized "marvels" had recently appeared on London stages—one at the Alhambra itself— and had subsequently been exposed as frauds. The so-called "bulletproof man" had been proved to be quite mortally vulnerable to bullets unless he was wearing his secret bulletproof vest; and the slender attractive girl who billed herself as "The Georgia Magnet," had claimed that by some "supernatural power" she could withstand the laws of gravity: five strong men could not, together, lift her from the stage. She had starred impressively on the Alhambra bill until an ingenious newspaper reporter learned and published the secret of her power: a clever but completely natural application of the laws of levers made it impossible for the five men to elevate her from the floor when they grasped her in the specific manner she insisted upon.

Slater's humiliation over the Georgia Magnet's exposure was too recent for him not to be wary of Houdini and his "marvelous" ability. Among the newsmen whom he nervously but wisely invited to the press showing was the reporter who had exposed her.

Houdini, writing about that tense scene long afterward, declared:

"That they were gunning for me is proved by the fact that the same newspaper investigator who exposed the Magnet, came upon the stage of the Alhambra at my press performance . . . and though he brought along an antique slave iron, which he seemed to think would put an end to my public career on the spot, I managed to escape in less than three minutes. When I passed back his irons, he grinned at me and said, 'I don't know how you did it, but you did!' and he shook me cordially by the hand."

The press performance was a success. But though it did not end Houdini's "public career," neither did it begin it, so far as the British were concerned. There remained his opening night to be survived, and Houdini was aware that neither the good will of the reporters nor Slater's confidence as expressed in his contract was a guarantee of a triumph. He still had the English public to win, and he must win it alone. Houdini was as near to nervousness as he had ever been in his life, as he paced the wings of the Alhambra stage on that eventful evening.

Finally his act was announced. The orchestra crashed into a loud march, and Houdini stepped forth. When he had reached the center of the stage the music was stilled.

"Ladies and gentlemen," Houdini said slowly and solemnly, "tonight I want to——"

"Stop!" A loud shout from the audience interrupted him. "I am the Great Cirnoc!" the voice continued, its bellow louder than ever as a huge burly figure leaped to the stage. "I am the original Handcuff King. This man is a fraud—an impostor!"

Houdini's amazement left him voiceless. Startled and uncertain, he stood without protest as the voice raged on. It accused Houdini of imposture in more than his profession: Houdini was not even an American, it insisted, and had not ever been in America.

The audience waited, tense but unsurprised. Another "marvel" was apparently undergoing the process of exposure.

But suddenly one member of that audience rose to his feet, and his calm voice cut authoritatively through Cirnoc's shouts.

"That is not true," it said decisively. "I know that the young man is an American. I am also from America, and I saw him several years ago doing his handcuff act there."

With an instantaneous change of mood, the audience burst into applause: the exposer himself was this time being exposed. They were delighted by the novelty.

Houdini, his composure recovered, stepped forward. "Get the Bean Giant," he whispered to Bessie as he did so. And Bessie, who had been standing like a small frozen image of fear, in her black velvet, lace-collared page suit, ran on trembling legs to obey. When she returned with the terrifying ponderous manacle that had been named for its Boston inventor, a Captain Bean, Houdini held it so that the audience might see. Then he turned to address Cirnoc—but his voice reached every person in the crowded hall.

"I'll give you five hundred dollars," Houdini challenged, "if you can get out of these cuffs."

Cirnoc glared at the irons and then at Houdini.

"Let me see you get out of them," he countered.

The audience was spellbound now. The sight of the irons themselves had caught at their imagination: they were far larger than the ordinary pair of cuffs, and looked particularly formidable. The Bean Giant had in fact been as effective as its appearance suggested: no one had ever succeeded in freeing himself from it until Houdini, not long before he left the United States, had mastered its secret.

Houdini was not afraid of the Bean Giant. Nor was he, any longer, afraid of Cirnoc. That unknown voice in the audience had given him back his courage.

"Lock me in," Houdini offered, thrusting the manacles into Cirnoc's hands and holding out his own wrists.

Cirnoc did a careful job. It took him some time to assure himself that the lock had snapped securely home. It took Houdini less time to disappear into his cabinet and step forth again, the cuffs dangling freely in his hand.

And this time, when Houdini challenged Cirnoc again to extricate himself from the Bean Giant, there was nothing else for the Original Handcuff King to do but accept. The audience would not have allowed him to do otherwise.

Houdini snapped the cuffs on, and with a dramatic gesture, offered Cirnoc the key. The audience chuckled appreciatively. Even if Cirnoc freed himself as quickly as Houdini had done—

which was likely, since he possessed the key—
the young American would still have showed
himself the cleverer and more resourceful of the
two. Cirnoc disappeared into the cabinet, and
Houdini gestured to the orchestra to play.

Long moments passed. Now the chuckles from
the audience were louder and more numerous.
Finally, they merged into one great roar of
laughter.

And when Cirnoc stepped out of the cabinet at
last, his hands still securely clamped by the Bean
Giant, his face red with fury, his tongue barely
able to twist itself around the bitter request that
Houdini release him—then the audience burst into riotous applause and shouts of congratulation.

Houdini bowed stiffly, from the waist. But
even his formal manner could not put them off.
They had just crowned a new Handcuff King,
and they considered his arrogance only fitting.

The quiet man in the audience who had given
Houdini the time and the confidence he needed
in that black moment, smiled in the darkness. He
was a king himself, in the world of finance. His
name was Chauncey Depew.

And Harry Day, that young man whose
youthful inexperience had not prevented him
from recognizing Houdini's potential kingship
—Day also felt like a king that night. He knew
instinctively that his star would rise with Houdini's—as indeed it did—but he could not then

117

know that he would eventually become one of England's wealthiest, most successful business men, and a member of her Parliament. It was enough to know that he had picked a winner that night.

And that he knew without doubt. They were still applauding out there—they wouldn't let Houdini go.

Bessie had stars in her eyes and a lump in her throat. They hadn't conquered the world yet— but they had certainly conquered its largest capital.

10

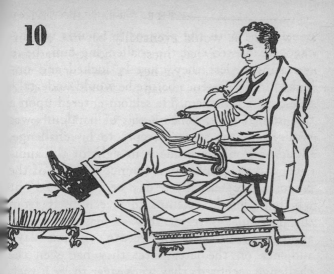

Overnight, Houdini became a topic of excited discussion throughout London. Slater, fully confident now of Houdini's ability, advertised him as an expert who challenged all comers, who stood willing to defy any restraint with which he might be tested. While Day busied himself booking his new client for a tour in Germany, crowds stormed the Alhambra. And among the merely curious and admiring at every performance, there was always a number of amateur or professional detectives, inventors, mechanics, and policemen, all bearing fetters which—they hoped—would defeat Houdini for their own glorification.

Houdini met them all, but with care and an increasing sense of showmanship. Mindful of his one failure with the plugged handcuffs in Chicago, he insisted that the challenging cuffs be in operating order: they must be locked and unlocked in his presence before he would undertake to escape from them. He seldom entered upon a test immediately. When a pair of handcuffs was brought to the stage in reply to his challenge, Houdini would examine it in sight of the audience, and then publicly announce the date of the performance—usually a day or two ahead—at which he would attempt to free himself from this particular restraint. It was a masterly device, almost guaranteeing the return of that day's audience on the later date: they had seen the challenge accepted; they were eager to see it met. The Alhambra's attendance record mounted daily, and Houdini's original two-week booking was stretched to four.

He could have remained even longer—Slater wanted to keep him—but he could no longer postpone the German engagement. Before he left London, however, he conferred with Harry Day, and then sent a cable to his brother Theo. It said, in effect, "Come on in. The water's fine!" The two Harrys had agreed that there was room for another Handcuff King in England—at any rate, for another who knew Houdini's own secrets and could, like him, challenge the public effectively. Houdini's sense of family responsibility was never very far below the surface. If there was money

be made in the handcuff-release business in
urope, he felt, it might as well be kept within
he Weiss circle. Shortly thereafter, young Dash,
laying under the name of Theo Hardeen,
rossed the Atlantic; and before the summer
nded the apparent rivalry between the two was
n added stimulus to the publicity for each. Har-
een, too, was warmly accepted by the British
nd was long to remain one of their favorite per-
ormers.

At the Central Theater, in Dresden, where
Houdini made his first continental appearance,
e more than repeated his London success. In
act, the cautious manager, Herr Kammsetzer,
far forgot his natural suspicion of importa-
ions as to dash on stage at the end of Houdini's
irst performance and lead the audience in wild
pplause. Day after day the Central's box office
ecords were smashed, and soon Herr Kamm-
etzer asked for an extension of the engagement.
t was impossible, Houdini told him: he was
ooked for the following month at the great
Wintergarten, in Berlin. Kammsetzer wrote to
Berlin and begged their indulgence. Berlin re-
used. If Houdini was that good, the Wintergarten implied, why should Berlin be unneces-
arily deprived of his appearance?

So Houdini played the next month in Berlin—
nd the Wintergarten's receipts soared higher
han they ever had before. Soon the Winter-

garten in turn was pleading for an extension, and again Houdini shook his head: Day had booked him next at the Ronacher Theater, in Vienna. But the Wintergarten was now as insistent upon keeping Houdini as it had been upon obtaining him in the first place. It calmly forwarded to Vienna the amount of Houdini's salary there— 4,000 marks for the month—and Houdini remained on the Wintergarten's stage throughout November.

The Houdinis were riding the crest of a high wave, but it was a wave which, by late fall, gave no evidence of breaking. Bessie had long ago forgotten the fear that tortured her in London— the fear that the Alhambra engagement, like their one week at Tony Pastor's and their one brief tour of the Keith circuit, would lift them up only to drop them again with a sickening thud. Now they were being offered more engagements than they could possibly fill. The future was no longer obscure; it was illuminated— brilliantly illuminated far ahead. There was still a great deal of work to do. Houdini had an assistant now and was soon to have several more, but these added to Bessie's responsibilities rather than decreased them: it was she who had to look after their well-being when Houdini drove them too hard or found fault with them unreasonably. And she was always on hand, whether she was needed on the stage or not, to keep their properties in order and attend to the thousand minute details surrounding a performance. Nevertheless, she felt that she could relax now, safe in the knowledge that their triumph was no longer a dream, but a solid and tangible thing.

Houdini himself, however, although as certain as Bessie that his star had risen at last and would remain high, never for a moment allowed himself to relax. Each evidence of his success seemed to resolve itself into new bursts of energy and inventiveness on his part.

No spectator ever knew ahead of time exactly what he would see when Houdini stepped out on the stage. One night he might be tied in intricate bonds of rope; the next would see him twisting out of tortuous chains and leg irons; on the third he might be nailed into a sturdy packing case by volunteers invited from the audience itself.

Whenever he entered a new city he went straight to the police headquarters, to challenge the authorities to lock him in their strongest fetters and their safest prison cell. Not once did he fail to escape, although each succeeding city attempted to outdo the others by providing Houdini with more and more difficult restraints. All this was the most delectable fare for the public. In Germany, and elsewhere in Europe, the police were regarded as masters of the people rather than their servants; and it immeasurably tickled the fancy of repressed populations each time this stocky young man defeated attempts of the police to repress his person. Reporters regularly and happily followed Houdini to each jail, helped to strip and search him, and afterward wrote with enthusiasm the stories of his triumph.

The police themselves, of course, were not ordinarily so delighted with this "Elusive American," as he was beginning to be billed. In Hanover, for example, where Houdini shrugged off the heaviest manacles as easily as a dog shakes itself dry, the chief of police, Count Schwerin, was distinctly annoyed.

"Of course," he said, "iron fetters must be locked, and locks can be picked by a clever man."

Houdini bowed formally, as if he had been complimented. His public generally suspected that he used lockpicks for his work, but no such instrument had ever been discovered on him. The mystery therefore was perpetually intriguing: how *did* he do it?

"It is probable that nowhere else in Germany," Count Schwerin continued, "is there a restraint that will hold you. Here in Hanover, however, we have something that will do so."

"Let me try it," Houdini suggested.

"I do not think it would be wise." The Count smiled with kindly superiority. "It is a strait jacket for those prisoners who are too violent. You might break your bones in such a struggle."

"Let me see it."

Houdini had not done a strait-jacket release for a considerable interval, but he had mastered several examples of such restraints in the past—and, furthermore, he believed that such an escape was one of his most effective. He was more than willing to silence this pompous chief by another and particularly striking evidence of his skill.

But when the garment was put into his hands, his determination faltered. It was constructed of heavy canvas, and so strongly and completely reinforced with stiff leather that he could scarcely bend it enough to examine all its parts.

He recovered in an instant, however. He had never yet backed down on a challenge, and he did not intend to begin now.

"I'll try it," he said, a little more quietly than usual.

At a gesture from Count Schwerin a group of grimly smiling policemen set to work. Slowly Houdini was trussed into the cocoonlike contraption. His arms were inserted in sleeves sewn shut at the ends, crossed and pulled around his body, and fastened at the back with straps and buckles so snugly—the policemen were enjoying their work—that Houdini could hardly breathe. A high leather collar held his head and neck almost motionless.

The following interval of struggle was one which Houdini never forgot. He always maintained, in his later writings, that a strait-jacket release was more or less unique in that it depended on no real "trick." Knowledge and sheer strength and ability were its secrets. First a little slack must be obtained—and Houdini was a lifelong master in the use of his powerful, well-controlled muscles to obtain the precious slack required in so many releases. Utilizing that slack, it was then necessary to force the arms up over the head, so as to bring the sleeve buckles within reach of the teeth, and thereby open them. Thereafter, it was possible—for Houdini's steel fingers, at least—to work through the canvas to unbuckle the straps that held the garment closed at the back. But the material and construction of the garment that day in Hanover made each smallest move in the process particularly difficult and painful.

Inside the jacket he was soon wringing wet, and his clothes were being pulled to tatters. For an hour and a half he worked, every muscle tortured and aching, desperately short of breath, exhausted in every tissue of his body. But at the end of that time he was free. His body was dark with bruises —but he had escaped! Hanover—and all Germany—rang with his praise.

Not long after the Hanover incident, however, Houdini did meet defeat—though in a different field and at the hands of a very different sort of adversary.

They had gone to Paris to fulfill a contract, and found themselves with a few days of leisure. Bessie set forth happily to look at the Paris shops, and Houdini started on an exploration of his own.

It was, actually, a sentimental pilgrimage: he meant to visit and adorn with a wreath the grave of his hero, Robert-Houdin. He had discovered that the French magician's widow was still living, and had sent her a formal request for permission to make this gesture of homage.

The reply he received startled and infuriated him. Mme. Robert-Houdin regarded this professional namesake of her husband's as a presumptuous upstart, and she made her attitude quite clear: Houdini had had no right to borrow the name in the first place; he had less right to add further luster to his fame by publicly associating himself with Robert-Houdin's memory. Her answer to his request was no.

The rebuff was not without some reason. Houdini had certainly intended to have reporters and photographers present when he visited the grave. He could scarcely move these days without attracting attention, and he was becoming extremely skillful at taking advantage of the potential publicity value of almost everything he did. But he was furiously angry nevertheless. By now the "borrowed" name of Houdini was itself famous. Had Robert-Houdin ever drawn such crowds as flocked to see the Handcuff King? Mme. Robert-Houdin should be grateful, Houdini thought, for what he chose to regard as a generous impulse on his own part.

Houdini did not say publicly that he was angry. He said instead that he was hurt. He spent his free time in Paris visiting magic shops and book shops, purchasing everything he could lay his hands on that pertained to the history and practice of magic. A scholarly interest in one's profession could also be utilized as good publicity. But not long afterward, when his research turned up evidence that many of Robert-Houdin's "inventions" had actually been developed by earlier performers, Houdini began to collect material for a book which he eventually wrote—a book called *The Unmasking of Robert-Houdin*. He said that he felt it was "his sacred duty to revise the history of his craft, to uncrown the French conjurer . . . to credit the great triumphs of conjuring to dead and gone magicians whose glory Robert-Houdin had so unscrupulously pilfered."

There were differences of opinion as to his true purpose in publishing the book, but it must certainly be true that Houdini's feelings had been deeply injured by Mme. Robert-Houdin's attitude and by his own sense of disillusionment. He came to feel that he had for years modeled himself on—had even named himself for—a man now proved unworthy of emulation: Robert-Houdin had not been the great originator his autobiography claimed him to be. Only by exposing his onetime hero, Houdini perhaps felt, could he rid himself of the stigma now clinging to that association.

And however confused his motives, his enthusiasm for research in the field of magic was undeniable. From the time he began to earn any sizeable income at all, he always spent a considerable part of it on books and other materials to add to a rapidly-growing collection. Despite his lack of education he must have had something of his father's zest for scholarship.

But, probably *because* of that lack, the scholarship must always be publicly recognized. The Great Houdini had to be great in more ways than one—a great historian as well as a great magician, an authority in his field as well as one of its highest-paid performers. Throughout his life, in whatever city he was appearing, he visited old retired magicians and persuaded them to talk to him. He tracked down magicians' graves and made careful note of their dates. The publicity that usually attended these pilgrimages (none was ever again frustrated, as his visit to Robert-Houdin's grave had been) did not prevent him from being generous—and often secretly so—to down-and-out conjurers and has-beens of all kinds. He never saw a magician's unkempt grave without arranging for its immediate care.

The same earnestness that had at the age of twelve made him assume responsibility for his mother, now made him take responsibility for his entire craft. Other magicians sometimes thought he took too much on himself—that he spoke (as he frequently said he did) for "the profession," without the profession's permission—but Houdini believed that he was merely fulfilling a predestined obligation.

The beautiful dream had finally come true. Houdini was at last in truth Houdini the Great. Applauding thousands daily proclaimed the judgment. Houdini himself found the judgment accurate.

11

Only one thing was lacking to make his European triumph complete: his mother must witness it. When he and Bessie had been abroad for six months, Houdini began to make plans for bringing Mrs. Weiss over for a visit.

There wasn't a great deal of money in their account. Houdini always stayed at simple inexpensive lodgings and ate simple inexpensive food —indeed, he seldom seemed to notice where he lived or what he ate, and Bessie had to beg him to replace a tattered suit with a new one. But his income had not yet risen as high as his fame, and Houdini let money slip swiftly through his fingers, for books, for charity, for new equipment. He would buy an entire library as readily as a single volume. The extravagant gesture was natural to him. He was about to make one of his most spectacular ones.

He was walking down a London street one day in January of 1901—a street draped in heavy mourning for the beloved Queen Victoria who had died several days before—when he saw in a shop window the model of a gown that had been designed for Her Late Majesty. An instant later he was inside the shop, asking the price of the gown.

The astounded shop manager glared—and refused to sell. A royal memento could not be purchased. But people didn't resist Houdini very long when he was determined, and now his two strongest traits were uppermost: that of the showman, and that of the devoted son. For fifty pounds and the promise that the gown would never be worn in England, he had his way and left with the garment under his arm. A letter was promptly dispatched inviting Mrs. Weiss to join them at Houdini's expense and promising her a magnificent treat when she arrived.

The Houdinis were appearing in a theater in Hamburg when she reached them. It was a special benefit performance, and the house was completely sold out at fantastically high prices. Houdini announced that he wanted a seat for his mother that night, and the manager said it was impossible: there were no seats.

"I don't want *any* seat," Houdini went on, as if he had not heard. "She must sit in a box."

"Impossible," the manager intoned.

"Impossible?" The deep-set eyes grew dangerously bright. "If it is impossible to get her a box seat, it will be impossible for me to perform."

The manager cajoled, then pleaded, then threatened. Contractual obligations were pointed out. Houdini remained silent. He knew—and the manager knew—that the audience would be satisfied with nothing less than his appearance that evening. The other acts were merely unimportant preliminaries to the star turn. The manager capitulated.

That night Mrs. Weiss was present, seated in a chair that had been placed in one of the stage boxes. When Houdini received the kind of ovation he had always promised her he would win one day, it would be difficult to say which of them was more proud. It was a magnificent moment for both of them.

Immediately after the performance the Houdinis whisked Mrs. Weiss onto a night train for Budapest—the city from which the little Weiss family had fled in near-disgrace so many years before. There Houdini went directly to the most fashionable hotel and explained that he wished to hire its grandest salon for a private party. Once more he encountered an adamant manager—that salon was not available to private parties—but once more he prevailed. He did more than that: when the manager was informed of Houdini's plan he urged the American to accept the use of the room without payment.

Under Houdini's watchful eye his mother was dressed in the queenly robe that night and enthroned upon a great chair which had been placed at one end of the salon. And then the doors were opened and Houdini's guests came in. He had invited all of Mrs. Weiss's relatives, and any friends or slightest acquaintances who might once have thought of her as a poor emigrant seeking haven in the New World. Now, with the Great Houdini's permission, and in the magnificent setting he had devised, they were all permitted to pay their respects to the plump little woman who was suddenly a queen.

Houdini had promised his father that he would take care of his mother. He was keeping that promise with a magnificence that all Budapest would long remember.

Mrs. Weiss left the next day, tears of happiness standing in her gentle eyes. Houdini himself was transfigured. He scarcely noticed the fact that he had to borrow money for his and Bessie's fares on the train that carried them back to their work and to a further succession of triumphs.

The names of the cities the Houdinis took by storm during the next several months read like a guidebook of the major centers of Europe: Leipzig, Frankfort on the Main, Magdeburg, Dortmund, Bochum, Osnabrück, Cologne, Copenhagen. Part of the time he traveled as a star with the famous Corty-Althoff Circus, and its success that season was laid largely to his drawing-power. The Circus had recently lost all its horses and—as Houdini himself wrote—"in Germany a circus without horses is no circus." But in Germany that year, a circus with Houdini was the greatest attraction that could be offered.

Houdini had not been the first handcuff king, but now he resented all those who had come before and after him. He was aware that it was a measure of his own superiority when many of them, in an effort to impress the public, claimed to have bested even the Great Houdini himself. But he could never let such claims go unchallenged.

One German, a man named Kleppini, insisted that he had escaped from all of Houdini's fetters, but that Houdini had failed to release himself from the cuffs Kleppini used. When Houdini heard of the claim he instantly obtained a temporary release from Corty-Althoff, and dashed from Holland—where he had been appearing—to Dortmund. When he arrived at the theater where the German was playing he paused long enough to disguise himself with a false mustache and then he went inside and found an unobtrusive seat. He sat quietly until Kleppini launched into his usual speech describing the nonexistent occasion when he, Kleppini, had vanquished the Elusive American.

"Not so!" Houdini shouted suddenly.

Kleppini paused, reddened, and demanded to be told how the interrupter could make such a statement.

Instantly Houdini leaped upon the stage, tore off his disguise, and thundered, "Because I am Houdini!"

The audience burst into shouts and applause. "A test! A test!" someone called out, and immediately the cry was taken up.

Houdini was delighted. This was just what he had been hoping for. "I dare you to let me lock you up," he challenged Kleppini. "Here are five hundred marks which are yours if you can escape."

Kleppini hemmed and hawed and refused to answer. The audience's shouts became jeers, but Kleppini still resisted. Houdini finally left the stage in triumph.

But not many hours later Kleppini's manager visited Houdini at his hotel to make formal arrangements for a test. During the conversation he examined Houdini's various fetters, expressing particular interest in a French letter cuff. This could be opened only when the disks of its lock were rotated in such a way that the letters on their many faces spelled out a particular word. According to Houdini, who later reported the conversation, the manager asked transparently obvious questions about the cuff, and Houdini answered him in similar vein. Swearing the manager to secrecy, Houdini told him that the combination word was *clefs*, the French word for *keys*. The contest was finally arranged for the following evening, and all the next day men wearing huge posters marched up and down the streets of Dortmund announcing the event.

The two performers appeared on the stage. Kleppini immediately cast a quick glance at Houdini's fetters, chose the letter cuff, and hurried into his cabinet to examine it in privacy. When he emerged he announced that he would meet Houdini's challenge by opening this cuff—admittedly one of Houdini's most difficult. Houdini smiled, examined the cuffs himself, and finally locked them in place. With assurances to the audience that he would be out in a moment, free, Kleppini then permitted himself to be shut in his cabinet.

Houdini's upraised hand silenced the roll of music from the orchestra. "Ladies and gentlemen," he said, "you may all go home. I do not lock a cuff on a man merely to let him escape."

The audience applauded, but had no intention of leaving until the performance was over.

Minutes went by. Kleppini was still in his cabinet. The manager, sensitive to a swiftly-rising wave of impatience, declared that the rest of the

acts would now appear. And appear they did—
performing to the left and the right of the still-
shut cabinet where Kleppini worked. The last
act was finally concluded, and still Kleppini had
not emerged. The audience accepted Houdini's
verdict with a handsome ovation, and finally it
too was gone. The enraged manager then ordered
that the cabinet be carried bodily off the darkened stage.

At twelve-thirty that night, Houdini was visited by Kleppini's weeping wife, begging him to
release her husband. Houdini summoned reporters and took them to the office where Kleppini,
convulsed with rage and frustration, showed the
letters of the cuff turned to form the word *clefs*.

Houdini smiled at him pityingly. "Didn't
you guess," he asked, "that I would change the
combination before I locked them on? Here." He
manipulated the letters. "There—now they spell
a good American word that means Kleppini."

As he spoke the bracelets fell off. The letters
had been twisted to spell out FRAUD.

But it was not always quite so easy as that to
maintain his title of King of the Handcuff Kings.
In Blackburn, England, in the fall of 1902, Houdini attempted to release himself from fetters
supplied by a Mr. Hodgson, the principal of a
school of physical training. It appears that Houdini had not, in this case, seen the irons beforehand, and when he examined them on the eve-

ning of the test—in a theater crowded "literally from floor to ceiling," as the Blackburn *Star* declared—he claimed that they had been tampered with. The lock had been wrapped around with string, he remarked, and otherwise altered to make escape more difficult. Hodgson replied firmly that he had fulfilled the regulations of the test, which had simply stipulated that he bring his own irons.

"I insist that you have gone beyond the terms of the challenge," Houdini stated. And then, turning to the tensely expectant audience, he added, "But of course I am quite willing to undergo the test, provided you will allow me a little extra time in which to deal with these unusual difficulties."

The audience cheered the sporting decision, and Hodgson stepped forward to fasten the irons in place. The *Star's* report of that process suggests the drama of the scene:

". . . Mr. Hodgson, with the aid of a companion, fixed a pair of irons over Houdini's upper arms, passing the chain around his back and pulling it tight, and fixing the elbows close to the sides.

"To make assurance doubly sure, he fixed another pair in the same manner, and padlocked both behind.

"Then, starting with the wrists, he fixed a pair of chained 'cuffs' so that the arms, already pulled stiffly behind, were now pulled forward. The pulling and tugging at this stage was so severe—the strong man exercising his strength to some purpose—that Houdini protested that it was no part of the challenge that his arms should be broken. He also reminded Mr. Hodgson that he was to fix the irons himself.

"This led to Mr. Hodgson's assistant retiring.

"Proceeding, Mr. Hodgson fixed a second pair of 'cuffs' on the wrists and padlocked both securely, Houdini's arms being then trussed to his sides so securely that escape seemed absolutely impossible.

"Still Mr. Hodgson was not finished with him.

"Getting Houdini to kneel down, he passed the chain of a pair of heavy leg irons through the chains which bound the arms together at the back. These were then fixed to the ankles, and after a second pair had been added, both were locked and now Houdini seemed completely helpless.

"A canopy being placed over Houdini in the middle of the stage, the waiting began, and the excitement grew visibly every minute. . . ."

In these days of rapid-fire entertainment, it is difficult to appreciate the gravity with which audiences sat out the kind of endurance contests which Houdini's performances frequently became. The scene in Blackburn that night was

often echoed elsewhere. When, at the end of fifteen minutes, Houdini asked that the canopy be raised, the audience burst into shouts of approval —shouts which subsided immediately when their hero was revealed lying helpless on his side, still completely bound. He asked to be lifted up, and Hodgson refused. At that the audience shouted again, but this time in fury against Hodgson, for his unfair treatment of the challenger. Despite Hodgson's protests, Houdini was lifted to his knees, the canopy was lowered again, and again the audience sat in tense expectation.

Twenty minutes later Houdini once more had the canopy raised. He explained that his arms were bloodless and numb, and asked that the cuffs be removed long enough to allow the circulation to be restored. The *Star* reported that "Mr. Hodgson's reply, given amidst howls, was 'This is a contest, not a love match. If you are beaten, give in.' "

The audience was close to violence. A doctor stepped forward to examine Houdini, declared that "his arms were blue, and that it was cruelty to keep him chained up as he was any longer," but Hodgson remained firm. Houdini said steadily that he would continue and the audience screamed approval.

At the end of another fifteen minutes he announced that one hand was free. This brought the audience to its feet, and they remained stand-

141

ing and cheering while Houdini continued to work, reporting his progress as one iron after another gave way. At last—shortly after midnight, a little more than two hours after he had been bound up—Houdini for the last time stepped forth from the canopy to throw the irons down on the stage.

His clothing was in shreds, and his lacerated arms were bleeding. "The vast audience stood up and cheered and cheered, and yelled themselves hoarse to give vent to their overwrought feelings," the *Star's* reporter wrote excitedly. "Men and women hugged each other in mad excitement. Hats, coats and umbrellas were thrown up into the air and pandemonium reigned supreme for fifteen minutes."

Each event of this nature enormously increased the demand for his appearance. Day could scarcely keep track of the requests for bookings. By the latter part of 1902, Houdini was sometimes receiving not only an extremely high salary, but also a share of the theater's profits during the week or more of his billing there. He frequently earned £250—some $1200—a week, at a time when whole families were living on as little as $18 weekly. Throughout England his name was invariably the signal for spectators to pack a theater to the doors; throughout western Europe he was equally popular. When a German police officer, one Werner Graff, published an article claiming that Houdini was a fraud—that all his escapes were managed by bribery or some similarly dishonest means—Houdini was so confident of public support that he dared to charge the officer with criminal libel. To the delight of the public he won his case, despite the fact that Graff appealed the decision twice to higher courts. Houdini's bravado earned him as many admirers as did his skill.

And when, in early 1903, he crossed the border into Czarist Russia, it was again a combination of skill and bravado that brought him nationwide popularity. He refused to be satisfied with the menial role then allotted to performers in that country, and thereby won the respect of the nobility as well as the adoration of the general population. In Moscow, in St. Petersburg—now Leningrad—and at the famous annual fair at Nizhnii Novgorod, he drew enthusiastic crowds. He gave a command performance before the Grand Duke Sergius, whose gift to him Houdini proudly reported as "a heavily bedecked ladle, used in olden times to fill the glasses with champagne. It is valued at 1,000 rubles. This will stand alongside the silver bowl that I received in Essen Ruhr for breaking all records for paid admissions in the Rhine Province." His earnings during this period also reached a gratifying new high: in one week he was paid the equivalent of $1,750.

But England was clamoring for him again, and

Houdini returned across Europe to sweep once more through the British variety halls. Only once there did the challenges he continually accepted bring him to the verge of disaster, and that was when he was invited by *The Illustrated Mirror* to pit his skill against a pair of handcuffs the newspaper had obtained especially for the purpose. These manacles had been designed and made by a skilled locksmith who had devoted five years to the task. Their lock was novel and intricate. And, in addition, the two bracelets were separated by a length of pipe instead of the usual chain; the prisoner's two hands could not touch each other. For this reason alone, apart from the peculiar design of the lock, the newspaper's publisher and many consulting experts believed that Houdini's fabulous record was about to be broken at last.

Four thousand people jammed London's huge Hippodrome on the afternoon of the test. At a few minutes after three o'clock, Houdini, the irons locked around his wrist, disappeared into his cabinet. Several times after he emerged, to premature shouts of congratulation. Once he merely desired a better light than the cabinet afforded; once he wished only to flex his weary muscles. The third time he asked to have the cuffs removed briefly in order that he might take off his coat. The newspaper's representative politely refused; he knew that if Houdini were to witness the unlocking of the cuffs, he would inevitably learn something of their secret. The audience booed the decision; Houdini, perfectly aware of the reason behind the refusal, nodded agreeable acquiescence. But before he returned to his cabinet he wriggled around until he was able to extract a penknife from his vest pocket and open it with his teeth. Then he deftly slid his coat up over his head, slit it to ribbons, and shrugged off the remnants. When he disappeared once more he had been manacled for an hour.

The audience was tense. Shouts of encouragement to Houdini sounded from here and there, and occasional calls advised him to give up. In accordance with the custom of the period, the theater management had scattered through the crowd hired groups of young men whose job it was to keep excitement at fever pitch by expressing their encouragement to the apparent loser. It is doubtful if they were needed that day. The *Mirror* had naturally aroused considerable faith in its widely-publicized handcuffs, and there was a strong feeling everywhere that this time Houdini might actually fail.

But within ten minutes after the removal of his coat he emerged once more, this time with the loose cuffs swinging in his hands.

"A mighty roar of gladness went up," the *Mirror* gallantly admitted in the story describing its own defeat. "Men waved their hats and shook

145

hands with one another. Ladies waved their hand-kerchiefs, and the committee, rushing forward as one man, shouldered Houdini and bore him in triumph around the arena."

Houdini had done it again. In seventy minutes he had opened the manacles that had required five years to manufacture.

12

Nothing was impossible now, Houdini thought —including his dream of being one of the greatest stars on the American stage. He had planned to return home when managers in the United States would be willing to pay him their highest salaries. Now that time had come.

He felt sure that they knew about his European exploits: he had, characteristically, seen to it that they should know. He had been including accounts of his triumphs in the long chatty letters he wrote regularly to *The New York Dramatic Mirror,* the leading theatrical newssheet of the day, and the *Mirror* had been printing the letters as often as they were received. Actually his own name appeared only seldom in the news-packed paragraphs chiefly devoted to the other performers Houdini had encountered in the cities he was visiting. He reported on American acts in Europe, and described the best—and sometimes the worst—of the European acts he saw. Sometimes he was bombastic: in one of his earliest notes he gravely cautioned American performers against coming to Europe without having previously obtained bookings there. The Continent was crowded with top-flight performers, he warned; it was foolhardy to risk starvation by arriving without assurance of work. He was careful not to add that this was precisely what he had done himself.

But his praise was generous, and his condemnations brisk and pointed. He saved his harshest words for those whose acts were imitative—as he saved his own hardest feelings for those who attempted to imitate him. He was informative. He was readable. The references to his own successes were not permitted to destroy the news value of his letters. But he knew those references must have been noticed. In December of 1903, when he saw the *Mirror's* big holiday issue, he was sure of it: on the page where the *Mirror* saluted

American performers abroad—including Smith & Doreto, the eccentric comedy team; O.K. Sato, the juggler, said to have been the first American to make Europeans laugh; and W. E. Robinson, who dressed in Chinese costume and billed himself as the Chinese conjurer, Ching Ling Soo— on that page Houdini's own photograph appeared. And the *Mirror* described him as the Handcuff King, "too well-known to need any introduction to *Mirror* readers, as his bright and entertaining letters from Europe are a regular feature of the paper."

So, on the whole it seemed reasonable enough to Houdini, in the spring of 1904, to assume that America was ready for his return. Houdini told his agent, young Day, that he would not be available for European bookings that summer and autumn; gathered together the boxes of old books and other magical lore he had collected; and purchased passage home. Even his customary bout of seasickness on the way couldn't dampen his triumphant spirits.

His mother, of course, was overjoyed to see him. The Weiss family celebrated magnificently. And the agents whom he shortly visited seemed equally happy; they immediately offered him several circuit engagements for the coming season.

But the offers didn't quite satisfy Houdini. The reason was not simply that the salary mentioned was less than he had been receiving abroad. Money in itself had no interest for him, and if American standards had been generally lower, he would not have minded the reduction. It was true, on the whole, that European managers paid better than the American ones, in those days. It was also true that a few highly successful performers in the United States were receiving more than the agents were now bidding for Houdini. And that was the fact that struck him most forcibly.

American magicians were, at that very time, beginning to emerge from obscurity into a leading place among the magicians of the world. But for the moment they were more likely to be popular elsewhere than in their own country. New York, for example, had no theater devoted purely to magic, such as the one Maskelyne and Devant were successfully operating in London; New Yorkers weren't sufficiently enthusiastic about the conjurer's art. And although W. C. Fields, a morose young American juggler, was as widely popular at home as he was in Australia, a magician was seldom so fortunate. The phenomenal popularity of T. Nelson Downs—the King of Koins—was not considered a guarantee that another magician could fare equally well.

Moreover, the agents felt that the success of Downs—or any other magician—was not relevant in Houdini's case. He was not a magician, in the ordinary sense. He called himself an "escape artist"; the trade called his act a "novelty."

And novelty acts were notoriously the least predictable commodity in the world. Their successes were sometimes spectacular, but their failures were on an equally grand scale. Thus, American agents were, in their own opinion at least, merely using common sense when they offered Houdini a good but by no means enormous salary. And they thought they were being more than fair when they added that they would increase that salary at the end of his first season if Houdini had earned the public's approval.

If he had earned public approval. . . . To Houdini's ears the polite phrase had the sting of an insult. He had said he would come home a star, and he had done so. But these pigheaded American agents—the very ones who had failed to appreciate him years before—still could not recognize his value. He replied to all their offers with a curt No, and turned his back on all their well-meant suggestions. With his most arrogant manner he explained that he had no further time to discuss the matter: Europe was begging for him, and he must return.

He cabled Harry Day that he would, on second thought, accept bookings abroad for the autumn. And for the remainder of what he now called his "vacation" in the United States, he devoted himself to personal matters.

He bought a house—a big brownstone on West 113th Street, in New York City—that was to be his home for the rest of his life; it was also to be the Weiss family headquarters. There Mrs. Weiss would be "taken care of," as young Ehrich Weiss had promised she would be, and there his brothers and sister should live for as long as they liked. It satisfied Houdini's deep sense of responsibility to provide thus for the entire family, and he meticulously observed what he considered to be his further duty to them by purchasing a family burial plot and having the bodies of his father and a brother reburied there. And then, his obligations completed, he turned to that only other interest which he found as "personal" as his family and even more absorbing: his profession, his magic.

The moment he took possession of the house, he began to transfer to it his constantly-increasing magic collection—a haphazard jumble of old and new books, old and new theatrical programs, valuable items, and items of little value to anyone except Houdini. Everything he had bought during the European trip was now proudly unpacked and installed in his library; very soon the boxes and piles of hoarded miscellany were overflowing into the cellar, attic, and various odd corners all over the house.

Houdini arranged it all himself, with laborious care. As he worked he described to his mother—or to anyone else who would listen—where he had found this old program; that rare copy of

Hocus Pocus, dated 1635; a certain much-prized photograph of the retired and long-forgotten magician, Wibjalba Frikell, who had so tragically died an hour before Houdini's own first meeting with him was to have taken place. Bessie had his meals served to him in the library during those settling-in days. Otherwise, Houdini would scarcely have eaten at all.

There was only one other room in the house in which he took any real interest. Housefurnishings were of no more concern to him than the food he ate. But he did spend considerable time and money on his bathroom, having it fitted with a tub large enough for him to submerge himself in—so that he could practise underwater feats—and with a wall-sized mirror before which he could watch himself during his practice hours, and thus detect the tiniest flaw in his performance.

No vacation, of course, was ever without its practice sessions. In fact, Houdini could not even spend an evening at home with friends without making some professional use of the time: he did coin manipulations while he talked, or nonchalantly removed his shoes and socks and, with his bare toes, tied and untied the knots in a length of twine, apparently unaware that others might find the performance distracting.

By mid-August the house was in order, the family provided for. And Europe was indeed—

With his bare toes, he tied and untied knots in a length of twine.

as he had assured the American agents—clamoring for his return. The Houdinis sailed back to England, preparatory to opening in early September at the Hippodrome, in Glasgow.

Houdini had done very well with his formula for success: "I, Houdini, challenge. . . ." But the public's reaction to the London *Mirror's* dare had suggested that there might be an even more spectacular version of this theme. From now on, he decided, he would not be the issuer of challenges, but, instead, the Davidlike accepter of whatever dares the world's Goliaths could invent. "I, Houdini, accept any challenge. . . ."

. . . Any challenge whatsoever, the phrase implied. And the implication was, to all practical purposes, true. If there ever was an escape challenge which Houdini did not accept, the world was never allowed to hear of it.

That night in the Glasgow Hippodrome he made the statement to a packed house. Two days later the manager of Lacki, Graham, and Company, a nationally-known harness manufacturing firm, challenged Houdini to extricate himself from a new strait jacket the company had just perfected. The challenge was accepted immediately; the night of the test announced. Before a record audience Houdini allowed himself to be strapped into the hideous garment—the company's representatives required fifteen minutes for their job—and in less than an hour, working in full sight of the audience, he was free.

Throughout the British Isles ingenious people in all walks of life, in all trades and professions, set their minds to the task of devising a restraint from which Houdini could not escape. The new version of the challenge appealed universally to men's pride in their own knowledge and workmanship, and took advantage of the very human love of personal publicity which Houdini himself so clearly understood.

A group of workmen in a packing box factory would dream of the acclaim that would be theirs if they were to defeat the so-far-undefeatable Houdini. A paper bag manufacturer would decide that Houdini could certainly not free himself from a paper bag without destroying the bag and thus forfeiting his success. Basket weavers, department-store package wrappers, trunk and bag makers, hospital attendants who had developed a high degree of skill at restraining violent patients by tying them with wet sheets, sailors whose intimate knowledge of knots convinced them that they could bind anyone beyond the possibility of escape—every town in which Houdini played offered at least one such group or one such individual eager to challenge Houdini's mastery. They all knew that their names would appear in the newspapers even if they failed, that they would in any event share Houdini's limelight at least briefly. And they all realized that if they were to succeed in their attempt they would become world-famous.

The challenges poured in, in a never-ending stream.

Houdini's acceptance of them followed what came to be a pattern. The challenge itself would be issued to his advance agent, or to the performer himself when he reached town. It would be presented formally from the platform, usually on the night of his first performance. At that same time Houdini would name the performance at which he would meet the test; usually the date he set was for a night or two later.

Until the test itself, the challenger's container would be on public view in the theater lobby—unless, of course, as in the case of a packing box, it was actually to be constructed around Houdini, on the stage and in view of the audience. In such situations Houdini reserved the right to specify certain details such as a minimum size, to prevent suffocation.

The townspeople would turn out to hear the challenge delivered by one of their own number, perhaps return the following night to make further study of this performer whom Birmingham —or Edinburgh or Stratford or Bristol—hoped to defeat, and then, usually, return on the night of the test itself, to cheer alternately for their fellow-citizens and for the champion who in-

CHALLENGE!

HARRY HOUDINI,

AVENUE THEATER, SUNDERLAND

Sir,

We, the undersigned joiners and employes have figured it out that the Trunk Trick you are doing IS NOT GENUINE, but is prepared (and hearing that you Escaped from the Cells at the Central Police Station in 3 minutes, when you were locked up by Superintendent Deighton on Monday night) we challenge you to allow us to make an ordinary Packing Case of One Inch Deal, into which we guarantee TO HAVE YOU NAILED AND ROPED up so that you CANNOT GET OUT without DEMOLISHING THE BOX.

If you do not care to try it publicly, will you try it privately, if so, let us know when to send the case and we shall be at your disposal.

J. Atkinson, 1 Collingswood St., J. Douglas, 11 Shakespeare St., W. Mason, 12 Carroll St., J. Melville, 5 William St., J. Trueman, 10 Gill Bridge Avenue

EMPLOYES AT MESSRS.

W. PICKERSGILL & CO.,

SHIPBUILDERS, SOUTHWICK

HOUDINI
ACCEPTS THE ABOVE CHALLENGE
FOR
WEDNESDAY NIGHT, MAY 24TH, 1905
AT THE AVENUE THEATER, SUNDERLAND
EVERYONE ALLOWED TO BRING HAMMER AND NAILS!

evitably emerged victorious. Record-breaking crowds were the rule rather than the exception wherever Houdini went.

Sometimes there were competing groups within a single town: a team of packers from the local shipping company, and a rival team representing a local box maker, each determined to outwit both the other team *and* Houdini. In such communities excitement ran particularly high.

One of the greatest problems for any performer is the constant necessity to keep his act new and fresh, to prevent it from bogging down into monotony. Houdini achieved this superbly well with his appeal for challenges. They were endless in number and wide in variety. His public was not a master demanding new tricks at every performance; it was his most eager assistant, daily providing the material for its own dramatic entertainment.

But Houdini's work was by no means easy. He had always to be on his toes, ready for anything that might come his way. He was ingenious at devising quick changes in plan if for any reason the program seemed to lag. He would combine two challenges and meet them simultaneously: he 'would permit the local police to manacle him and then, still manacled, permit himself to be locked or nailed or roped into whatever container the second challenge had specified.

His newspaper publicity never suffered from the fact that local persons had an important role in each of his performances, but Houdini paid for that publicity. Each of those persons—and they differed every day—was a separate challenge to his skill and his knowledge. The stories in the press about him were numerous and laudatory— but those stories would dissolve into nothingness if, just once, he failed to conquer a restraint that any member of his public had devised. Living beneath the sword of Damocles must have seemed to him, at times, a comparatively safe existence.

Early in 1905 a cable from America arrived, offering him a handsome six-weeks' contract at a figure which American managers had refused to consider a half-year before. Houdini replied briefly that he was booked through the summer and was therefore uninterested. But the casualness of his answer was no true indication of his feelings. He was triumphantly aware that the United States, too, was beginning to beg for him now.

"Good!" he told Bessie. "Let them beg a while. Let *them* see how it feels to wait—and wait some more."

He could not have left England then if he tried. His name was in British headlines every day; his arrivals, his triumphs, his departures, were news events of importance. Theater managers never had to rack their brains to devise advertisements for his appearances—the advertisements wrote themselves.

Houdini was part of the life of England. England had made him, and it held him fast.

But toward the end of July, 1905, he finally left. He had been offered the headline spot at the handsome Colonial Theater, in New York. He was returning to the United States this time on his own terms. He was going home a star.

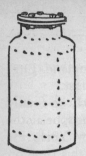

13

"The fame of his exploits in Europe had preceded his appearance, and everyone was on tiptoe to see the great 'Handcuff King' at work," a newspaper reported the morning after Houdini's early October opening at the Colonial. The theater was crowded, Houdini was at his authoritative best, the performance was a magnificent success. The acclaim was as enthusiastic as even Houdini could have wished. "The audience stared in blank amazement," the newspaper story declared.

Houdini had not prepared a special act for the occasion. To most American audiences, all his tricks were new, and he could play his repertoire over from the beginning. He presented handcuff releases—"several times during the week he was manacled by experts," a newspaper reported—and, "of a more startling nature than his handcuff work, a trunk trick which is by all odds the very slickest thing of its kind." The ovation awarded to that old stand-by, the "Metamorphosis," must have given Houdini a certain wry amusement; he had tried to present that performance in New York a dozen years earlier, but then only the dime museums would have him. The trick itself had not changed; the only difference lay in the aura of success that now surrounded it. Houdini was famous; therefore it must be good.

For the duration of his New York appearance he was the talk of the town. Afterward, on a Keith tour that took him to most of the major cities of the United States, he repeated the triumph in each. A typical Keith ad read:

WEIRD! MYSTERIOUS! INEXPLICABLE!
THE GREATEST DRAWING CARD
IN THE VARIETIES

At Washington, D. C., one of the first stops on his route, his jail-breaking skill called forth a challenge from the Warden of the Federal prison there. Houdini accepted, requesting that he be locked in the very cell which had held Charles J. Guiteau, President Garfield's assassin. Intrigued by its unusual lock—a combination with five tumblers—and by the intricate manner in which it was fastened not to the narrow door itself but to a metal bar protruding from it, Houdini felt that this cell presented peculiar difficulties. His mastery of it should therefore be particularly spectacular.

Stripped, searched, and locked in the cell, he was almost immediately free. But before he made his way to the Warden's office, where his judges were waiting, he exercised his skill on several other locks nearby.

"I let all your prisoners out," he announced calmly, as he walked, fully clothed, into the Warden's presence. His hearers stared at him, so amazed by his swift appearance that they hardly comprehended his words. Then as Houdini's statement penetrated their minds, the Warden and several guards leaped for the door.

"Don't worry," Houdini assured them. "I locked them all in again. In different cells."

The story skyrocketed through the press of the nation. There was not in this country the same mass hatred of the police which made Houdini's tricks in Europe so warming to the public's heart, but a colossal jest at the expense of the Federal penal system was nevertheless too daring a joke not to be enjoyed. Americans laughed with Houdini—and flocked to see him.

By no means a true prankster, he did on a few other occasions tickle the American sense of humor. Not long after the Washington event he was securely locked—stripped, searched, and heavily manacled as usual—in a cell of Boston's city jail. In the Warden's office the usual group awaited the outcome. Twenty minutes went by —far longer than Houdini ordinarily required for such a stunt—and the Bostonians began to congratulate themselves; perhaps they had succeeded where so many others had failed. Three minutes later the phone rang. Houdini was calling—from the Keith theater, a seven-minute drive away. He was not only free and dressed again in the clothes that had been locked in a separate cell; he was beyond the jail wall and halfway across the city.

The whole Keith tour was lit by periodic bursts of that sort—and by attendant publicity in all the papers of the country. As he had done in his early days in England, Houdini broke out of jails everywhere, and freed himself from manacles of every description. New England's famous witch cage—a heavily padlocked, latticed steel box, fitting tightly over the upper part of the body, and intricately woven with chains that attached the prisoner to it at many points—held Houdini captive an hour and a half. But the Boston audience that viewed his escape numbered its original three thousand when the long wait was over: not a person had left the theater. And Houdini held Boston his captive for eleven long weeks, although hold-overs of a single week were considered unusual there.

In the *Dramatic Mirror's* holiday issue that December, Houdini took a half-page ad, ostensibly

—and in keeping with the other professional ads in the paper—to extend the season's greetings to his fellow-performers. But the message begins, "I TOLD YOU SO," and continues in large black type:

WHEN IT WAS DISCOVERED THAT HOUDINI, "THE PRISON DEFIER," HAD BEEN BROUGHT BACK TO AMERICA AT A SALARY OF $1,000 WEEKLY, ALL THE "WISE-ENHEIMERS" AND SOCIETY OF KNOW-IT-ALL FELLOWS POLISHED UP THEIR HAMMERS, SAYING "GOLD-BRICK."
IT HAS NOW BEEN POSITIVELY PROVEN BEYOND ANY CONTRADICTION THAT HOUDINI IS THE HARDEST WORKING ARTIST THAT HAS EVER TRODDEN THE VAUDEVILLE STAGE!!
HE IS WORTH MORE THAN THE SALARY HE IS BOOKED FOR!!!!

At the very bottom, after an imposing list of his exploits, and quotations from several enthusiastic press comments, the ad concluded, as if in afterthought:

Merry Xmas and a Happy New Year to All.

It was a rather startling piece of braggadocio, even for the flamboyant world of vaudeville. But Houdini had waited a long time for recognition by his fellow-Americans. It would have been surprising if he had not relished it to the full when it arrived.

166.

Even his mother-in-law had capitulated to him. Bessie had had a brief illness and Houdini, aware that she missed her mother, had gone to Mrs. Rahner's house and informed her that he would not leave again until she consented to accompany him to her daughter's bedside. Mrs. Rahner had finally agreed, and from that time on she and Houdini were the best of friends.

Toward the end of the Keith tour, in fact, Houdini felt so secure in every respect that he decided to own and manage his own show. His fame had established him as an escapist, but he was determined to prove to himself and the world that he was also a consummate conjurer, an all-round magician of many skills. Against the advice of everyone who knew him, he organized a troupe, obtained bookings, and set out prepared to present a series of acts that would fill an entire evening.

He soon realized that his advisers had been right. Certain of the stunts Houdini staged on his new show were highly effective, but his manner was unsuitable to a program that demanded his presence for much of a two-hour performance. He had learned to dramatize his natural intensity and air of concentration so that each of his escapes seemed truly a last-moment reprieve from some terrible fate. But the sleight-of-hand tricks he now also insisted upon presenting suffered from this severity; they needed a lightness, a gaiety, that Houdini lacked. As the headline act on a vaudeville bill he always provided a breath-taking climax to an evening's entertainment—but an evening of breath-taking climaxes was too much even for the most stalwart audience. Houdini continued to attract his usual crowds, but their reaction disappointed him.

Furthermore, he hated having to concern himself with budgets and train schedules, and he had no patience for the minute tasks of keeping a troupe of performers satisfied and co-operative. The details of management were a constant irritation to him—and when he neglected them things went badly. Altogether he was glad when the tour was over. He knew it had been a mistake.

He was more pleased with the results of another private venture of that same year. In the spring of 1906 there appeared his first published work, a small volume entitled *The Right Way to Do Wrong,* which created a considerable stir. The book was devoted to the methods employed by pickpockets, housebreakers, cat burglars, and many other types of criminals, and its purpose was to advise readers how best to protect their persons, their homes, and their money from theft and injury. But his historian's zeal had led him to include so many ingenious tricks of which most criminals had never heard, that many honest citizens felt Houdini had, in effect, written a

textbook for thieves and hoodlums—a book
which would increase rather than decrease the
amount of successful crime.

Houdini was loudly attacked—and, of course,
was just as loudly defended. Arguments over his
book were many and violent. They pleased its
author, just as he had been pleased by the comment of that California police chief who had long
ago warned that should Houdini "turn out to be
a criminal" he would indeed be a "very dangerous
man."

The book sold well, too—and this was particularly gratifying to Houdini because he was doing
more and more writing as time went on. He had
a secretary now, just as he had technical assistants in his troupe, and he kept them all busy.
Much of his writing appeared in a magazine
called *The Conjurers' Monthly*. In a characteristic burst of temper, Houdini had inaugurated
the publication himself, and he continued to publish it for two years with characteristic energy.

When he had first returned to the United
States he had been angered by the attitude taken
toward him by *The Sphinx,* then the outstanding
periodical for magicians. Houdini had felt that
his European successes deserved lengthy notice in
its pages, and the magazine's editor, Dr. A. M.
Wilson, thought otherwise. Dr. Wilson offered—
insultingly, in Houdini's opinion—to publish the

Handcuff King's picture at the usual advertising rates.

Houdini's answer was *The Conjurers' Monthly*, in which he stated his personal opinion of Dr. Wilson with the frank rudeness of a small boy sticking out his tongue. "We admit," he wrote on one occasion, "that Harry Houdini spent two weeks in Kansas City, home of *The Sphinx* and Dr. Wilson, and carefully refrained from making the latter's acquaintance. A visitor to the zoological garden may approach a cobra's cage and study the creature, but that is no reason why he should be moved to come into personal contact with it." Dr. Wilson replied in equally colorful terms. Their feud was lively and of long duration —and ended as abruptly as it had begun, when friends finally brought the two together, and they discovered that their enmity had bred a sturdy mutual admiration.

Such an about-face was not unusual for Houdini, although he could maintain certain grudges untiringly, and he found *The Conjurers' Monthly* a useful weapon against cherished enemies. Horace Goldin, the magician who had snubbed young Harry in the old Kohl and Middleton Dime Museum days, was the object of numerous attacks in its pages. Once the magazine suggested editorially that "If Horace Goldin ever wrote a book on magic, it would read something like this: Iiiiii I I iiii and me, also III iiii i ii iiii I and I I I."

But the *Monthly* was a lively magazine, apart from the quarrels it carried on. Hardeen, still performing triumphantly in England, contributed news from the halls and theaters of the British Isles. Joe Hayman, Houdini's early partner and now a successful performer touring the world with his own act, Hayman & Franklin, also sent a regular column of vaudeville notes and gossip. There was a letter column in which readers' problems and queries were answered, a barter column, and a contest in which a cash prize was awarded for the best parlor trick.

By far the greatest number of pages was devoted to Houdini's own writings in the field of magic history and research. He had named his magazine for the *Conjurers' Magazine*, earliest recorded periodical for magicians, published in London, in 1791. Houdini's own first number described its forebear, and several other historic precedents, in an article full of scholarly data. And from then on Houdini published many similar articles and illustrations drawn largely from the collection in his own library. Readers were constantly being assured that Houdini was student and historian as well as top-ranking vaudevillian.

Several chapters of what Houdini originally called *Unknown Facts concerning Robert-Houdin* first appeared in the *Monthly,* until a publisher offered to present the material in book form. Houdini then reported this offer to his readers, printed no further chapters of the book (he substituted for them other historic material from his overflowing files), and began instead to advertise the forthcoming volume. "$250.00 reward!!" the ads announced, "to anyone who can bring a book which has taken so much time, energy, travel and money, with such authentic data regarding real magical inventions." The newly-titled *The Unmasking of Robert-Houdin* was declared to be the "first authentic history of magic," and the publisher's stated price of two dollars had been reduced to one ("Houdini Pockets the Loss!") so that the book might reach not only the "favored few" but the "great reading public."

The book appeared in the spring of 1908. It was widely reviewed—even by nonmagical publications—and both admired and condemned. Some magicians thought Houdini had performed an immeasurable service to their craft; others thought he had deliberately tried to increase his own stature at the expense of a fine French artist. Certainly the book was not ignored, and that would have been the only reaction which Houdini would have found unsatisfactory. He was more than satisfied with the results of his labors. Like his one-time hero, he was now recognized as both author and performer. Another long-cherished ambition had at last been fulfilled.

But with something of a shock Houdini realized, once the excitement of publication had died down, that he had, for the first time in his life, been allowing his secondary interests to harm his professional career. He had been so absorbed in his literary pursuits that he had been permitting his performances to take care of themselves. He had been accepting challenges, and the challenges had been numerous enough. American workmen, like their British counterparts, had been supplying Houdini with a regular flow of packing cases, paper bags, boxes, and containers of every description; in Toledo he made his way out of an enormous leather football tightly laced by experts; in Boston he escaped from an iron boiler; in Toledo, again, he slipped out of a zinc-lined piano box, within which he had been tied and bound in a chain.

But the American public was easily bored. In a land of such rapid technical development, in a land where whole cities, great railroads, huge industries, seemed to spring into being overnight, no single marvel, however impressive, could be granted more than its share of attention. Americans would look at anything new and novel, and Houdini had been that, for a time. Now the theaters where he played were less crowded, the managers less eagerly seeking his appearance. Agents who had once said that Houdini's "novelty act" could not develop a sustained popularity were nodding their heads complacently and pointing out that they had been right.

Houdini looked the facts in the face. Unblinded by the self-confidence which sometimes distorted his views, he now clearly recognized the fault as his own. His previous success had been built on persistent day-by-day hard work; he was now suffering the results of having neglected, even briefly, that program. "Is this week the first step toward oblivion?" he wrote in his diary, in Cleveland, where for the first time since his return he had appeared on a vaudeville bill as anything less than the headliner. "We shall see," he added, and went calmly to work.

"It is on trains that I get most of my ideas," he once declared. "I close my eyes while riding, and try to picture to myself what I, as a spectator, would like to see another man escape from."

A newspaper could speak slightingly of Houdini's ability to devise new tricks: "He believes in blowing his horn," one article about him stated, "and he doesn't think much about hiding his light under a bushel. When things are getting slack and he does not fancy the size of the type used in printing his name in the newspaper, he thinks up some 'death-defying' stunt and lo, he finds himself on the front page again."

But other performers, and Houdini himself, recognized that it was this single trait which accounted for the duration of his popularity. "People have sometimes suggested that I have a genius for this sort of thing, but I know that what I have is 'sense,' " he explained. "I mean that I am sensible enough to know that the minute you stop working at your job you begin to go backward. And I don't want to go backward."

He immediately discarded the possibility of further exploiting the handcuff release. His new stunt, if he were to think of one at all, must be something entirely novel. And it should, preferably, be dangerous—or appear to be so. Houdini had discovered that "it is the element of danger that interests people. People do not wish to see me killed, of course, but they are more interested in a stunt if they think there is danger attached to it. . . . Human beings don't like to see other human beings lose their lives; but they do love to be on the spot when it happens."

Weeks of concentrated effort followed the diary note written in Cleveland. Anything which resembled a packing case or any of the other boxes he had ever released himself from, would he felt, not be startling enough. A metal container was somehow more effective than a wooden one, and yet even metal boxes were. . . .

The idea came slowly, was many times revised, demanded long hours of work with his assistants before it was fully developed, and required weeks of special training on Houdini's part. But when it was at last ready, he felt sure that it had been worth the effort.

On the night of its first presentation there was an air of unusual tenseness in the theater. The stagehands and the other performers on the bill had heard a little of what Houdini planned to do, and their curiosity brought them crowding into the wings. The audience had been promised a new thrill, and it, too, waited expectantly.

Houdini appeared, bowed as usual, and then with his customary gravity asked that the new equipment be brought onto the stage. Necks craned, spectators rose half out of their seats—and there was a slight sigh of disappointment as a large metal can, resembling an overgrown milk can, was trundled into view.

But there were gasps of astonishment as stage-hands, in solemn parade, marched in from the wings with buckets of water and filled the can to overflowing. The usual committee volunteered with special eagerness when Houdini invited the audience to superintend his performance. The can was thumped and sounded, its narrow neck carefully examined. All agreed that it was just what it appeared to be: a heavy metal can, securely riveted, and full to the brim with water.

Houdini stepped to the edge of the stage.

"Ladies and gentlemen," he said slowly, "I will be handcuffed by your committee, lifted into this can, and the top will then be fastened on and locked with six padlocks. I will then endeavor to free myself." He held up a hand for silence. "But before I undertake the test, I should like to ask your co-operation during a little experiment. You know, of course, that it is possible to remain under water for several seconds at a time. I shall have to be under water considerably longer than that, however, to extricate myself from the restraints and—if possible—get out of the can itself.

"With your indulgence, therefore, I shall now be submerged in the can for a full minute. I will ask you to time me by your own watches. And I suggest that you attempt to hold your breath also for that period of time, as I shall be doing. Perhaps you have never thought how long a minute without air may seem. Are you ready, gentlemen?"

He turned to his assistants, who nodded soberly. All over the vast theater watches were withdrawn from pockets, and men and women stared with mounting nervousness as Houdini—who had disappeared for a moment and now returned in a bathing suit—was lifted from the floor and held over the can. It was clear that the neck was barely wide enough to take his body, and that he would be in an extremely uncomfortable and cramped position when he was forced down into the receptacle. Slowly he was lowered; water displaced by his body as he entered the brimming can splashed onto the stage.

When only his head remained in view he nodded once. Everybody looked at their watches, drew deep breaths in time with Houdini's own, and held them as he disappeared.

The seconds crawled by. Ten, fifteen, twenty . . . all over the theater little gasps and bursts of nervous laughter punctuated the silence, as men and women one by one gave up a feat beyond their endurance. Eyes bulged and faces grew red—and a final explosive sigh marked each individual's failure to meet Houdini's challenge. But Houdini remained out of sight. The interminable and painful length of a single minute was dramatically stressed for every member of his audience.

At the sixtieth second an assistant tapped on the can, and Houdini immediately emerged, drenched but smiling. He was violently applauded, but he merely shook his head—he had done nothing yet.

"If the committee will handcuff me," he said, standing again in the center of the stage, "I shall now attempt the actual test."

The audience sat motionless as the restraints were fastened to his wrists, and assistants replaced the water that had overflowed from the can. When the handcuffs were securely locked, Houdini tossed his long wet hair out of his eyes.

178

"I am ready, gentlemen."

More water splashed onto the stage floor as he was again lowered into the can. It made the only noise in the vast hall as Houdini's muscular body disappeared from sight. The heavy lid was clamped on, the six padlocks swiftly locked, and a screen shoved forward to conceal the can from view.

There was no band thumping out music to accompany this wait. It took place in a silence that deepened unbearably as the seconds ticked on. Ten, fifteen, twenty . . . thirty, forty, fifty. . . .

At the end of the minute there was a shudder through the crowd. Houdini could remain under water for a full sixty seconds: he had just proved that. But surely that was the longest any man could endure such a strain—and he had still not emerged.

Ten, fifteen, twenty . . . the second minute was now nearly half over. It seemed an endless time ago that Houdini had been submerged into his watery prison.

A stagehand carrying a large axe walked out from the wings, to stand motionless beside the screen.

Forty . . . fifty . . . sixty!

Houdini had been inside the can for two full minutes!

"He's fainted! Let him out!" A woman's hysterical scream split the silence.

The stagehand with the heavy axe stepped closer to the screen, but he didn't raise the axe, didn't strike.

Ten ... twelve ... fourteen ... on the fifteenth second of the third minute, the screen was suddenly pushed aside, and Houdini stood before them, dripping and breathless, but alive and free!

The applause was deafening, the shouts of mingled relief and admiration loud enough to be heard a block away.

With what the newspaper next day called "one of the most bewildering" feats he had ever performed, he had recaptured the attention of the entire country, and the headlines of its press.

After that evening no other name topped Houdini's on any vaudeville bill. He had regained his crown and, in fact, had planted it more firmly than ever on his broad brow. American managers refused to let so valuable a property leave the country, although Europe was again pleading for his return.

Finally, in midsummer of 1908, Houdini published the following paragraph in *The Conjurers' Monthly*: "Harry Houdini finds that he must sail to Europe on August 18, 1908, on the S.S. *Kaiser William II*, to fulfill engagements for which he contracted some years ago and which can no longer be postponed." The *Monthly* would be "discontinued for some time to come," he explained. Actually it was not reissued until long after Houdini's death. In 1945, with Theo Hardeen as Editor Emeritus, it entered upon a new life which Hardeen's own death, that same year, did not interrupt.

Perhaps Houdini suspected that the years to come would be too full of new interests, for him to resume a toy he had once enjoyed. At any rate he filled his final issue with pronouncements covering the entire field of magic and almost its full history, as if hastening to make declarations he might not again find the opportunity to publish:

PINCHBECK WAS THE GREATEST MAGICAL MECHANICIAN WHO EVER LIVED.

PINETTI WAS THE GREATEST MAGICIAN WHO EVER LIVED.

M. HARTZ TOOK MORE THINGS OUT OF A BORROWED HAT THAN ANY OTHER MAGICIAN.

J. N. HOFZINSER WAS THE GREATEST CARD TRICKSTER WHO EVER LIVED.

One after another he set his verdicts down, for his fellow-magicians and posterity. And he signed himself by the title he wished his readers to recall whenever his name was mentioned: "The First Authentic Historian of Magic."

He was perfectly willing to return to Europe now. He had accomplished what he had set out to do so many years before.

14

The twenty-fifth anniversary of Houdini's first appearance with Jack Hoeffler's Five-Cent Circus was celebrated in Berlin with a great dinner in the performer's honor. The occasion had an obvious significance: it meant that Houdini was unquestionably a public figure now—that everything that happened to him, everything that interested him, was automatically a matter of public interest.

Often the story of a successful man loses its drama once the success has been achieved; afterward the tale settles down into a repetitious account of repeated triumphs. And it is true that Houdini's triumphs, in the years following that victorious American tour, were repeated so regularly—back and forth across Europe, in the United States again, in Canada, and Australia—

that they too had a certain monotony. But Houdini's life itself was never monotonous. His perpetual curiosity and his persistently lively imagination were always leading him into new fields, both inside and outside his profession—and his public followed him everywhere. Its devotion was recaptured time and again by his new and ever more astonishing performances on the stage; and its amazed admiration was equally stirred by Houdini's startling off-stage achievements.

Some of these last were off-stage only in a literal sense; they were deliberately planned as publicity stunts, as come-ons for his show. Whenever Houdini arrived in a city bordering a lake or river, he jumped, heavily fettered, into the water —and sprang to the surface a few seconds later with his shackles loose in his hands. Sometimes he was locked or tied inside a heavy packing case, in addition to being handcuffed at wrists and ankles. These aquatic endurance stunts, especially those performed in ice-filled waters, frequently won him the stern disapproval of the police, which in turn increased the public's acclaim for their hero.

He brought new interest to his strait-jacket release by presenting it in mid-air. After Houdini had been laced into one of those tortuous garments, he would be hoisted up, by a crane, to hang suspended head down from a high bridge or the highest building in town, and there—it was a breath-taking sight for the gaping crowd below—wriggled himself free. Magnificently he tossed the restraint to the audience before he was again lowered to the ground.

In 1909 in Germany, Houdini saw his first airplane—a fragile unsteady contemporary of the Wright brothers' recently constructed machine. Immediately, of course, Houdini wanted one for himself. His mania for collection, his absorption in all ingenious mechanical contrivances, his by now almost instinctive sense of showmanship—all these combined to make his possession of an airplane imperative.

Bessie's protests were useless. In a matter of days he had purchased a Voisin plane for more than 20,000 francs, hired a French mechanic to assemble it and teach him to fly, and rented a house to serve as hangar. The crude wings and tail of the machine carried huge letters spelling out the name HOUDINI.

Houdini's career as an aviator consisted largely of pacing frantically up and down a field, waiting for the weather to clear. His first flight lasted but a moment, and was followed by two weeks of repair work on the plane, which had suffered from a too sudden landing. He had the opportunity for only a few more similarly brief excursions before he had to leave for Australia, but he insisted upon having the plane dismembered, crated, and put aboard his ship, and he took the mechanic along. In Australia, too, the weather was against him, but there the impetus to take up his plane was enormously increased.

Europe had already witnessed a number of what passed for flights in those days—usually a few uneasy minutes spent a few feet off the ground, and ending more often than not in serious damage to the plane if not to its pilot. Australia, however, had not yet witnessed a single aerial miracle—and there was a Wright plane at the field near Melbourne, also awaiting favorable weather conditions. Finally the latter made the attempt, only to crash in the very process of getting off the ground. Public excitement reached a fever pitch when Houdini announced that he would not be deterred from making his attempt.

Each morning Houdini was at the field early, and the crowd was there before him. Finally the weather broke. Houdini took his plane up three times: one flight lasted, amazingly, six and one-half minutes. A hastily organized aviation club presented him with a trophy to signalize the first

aeronautical event in Australia. Now Houdin
had a new title to add to that of historian, scholar
and performer: he was the first airman of Australia, and one of the first in the world.

Another similarly successful, though less spectacular, feat also marked that same trip to the
continent down under. Houdini's ship had
stopped at the Fiji Islands, and the passengers
were applauding the ability of the natives to dive
under water for tossed coins and come up with
the coins in their mouths. Perhaps the applause
for others was more than Houdini could endure;
perhaps he sincerely disliked seeing his fellow-
passengers hoodwinked. At any rate he announced that the natives caught the coins not
with their mouths, but with their hands, and
slipped the coins into their mouths just before
surfacing. To prove his point, he suggested that
the ship's passengers handcuff a native before permitting him to dive.

The natives objected. The passengers had no
particular desire to press the matter. But Houdini
declared that if any native were willing to com-
pete with him, he too would be fettered and they
would dive together for coins. Finally one Fiji
swimmer agreed. His hands were tied together
behind his back with cord (he had refused to
be shackled with cuffs), Houdini was handcuffed,
and they stood ready to dive. The captain tried
to stop the performance, explaining that the wa-

ters were infested with sharks, and that Houdini's light body would attract them. Houdini pooh-poohed the idea, demanded that two coins be thrown overboard, and he and the native dived in.

The Islander reappeared first—without a coin. Houdini emerged some time later, still handcuffed, and with both coins in his mouth. He had, of course, as he explained, removed the cuffs under water, caught the coins, thrust them into his mouth, and locked the cuffs back on before surfacing. He had also—and he took care that the press should know about it—publicly bested one of the famous Fiji Island swimmers in an underwater contest.

Back in England some time later, he caught public attention by appearing in another new role—that of defender of the public's rights. English theater managers, at that time, were practising an undeniable fraud upon the public —and, incidentally, upon performers—by canceling the appearance and the fee of headline acts for matinee shows. The cancellations were not previously announced, and the cheated audience believed the performers themselves responsible. An actors' association had already brought suit against the managers, but had lost the decision. Houdini decided to take matters into his own hands.

When the manager of the Holburn Theater,

where he was appearing at the time, notified him that there would be no Houdini performance at the following day's matinee, he accepted the decision without complaint. But the next day, when the posters advertising his appearance were still on display, Houdini called on the manager, indicated the promise implicit in the posters, and declared that he must go on. The manager refused.

Again Houdini seemed meekly to acquiesce. But when he left the office he went backstage, and waited in the wings until an interval between two acts. Then, before anyone could stop him, he walked out on the stage, gestured to the orchestra to stop playing, and addressed the crowd. He told them flatly that managers were always responsible for the nonappearance of headliners, and suggested that those who had come to the theater that day with the purpose of seeing him either demand a return of their admission or refuse to leave the theater until Houdini had been permitted to perform. Then he calmly left the stage.

The startled manager hastily took his place, but the audience refused to listen to his efforts at explanation. Finally, in despair, he ordered the show to continue from the point at which Houdini had interrupted it, hoping that the disgruntled crowd would forget its grievance before the entertainment was over. His optimism was unfounded. When the curtain fell and the lights went up, the house remained motionless. And almost all of the seats were still occupied when the evening show began—making it impossible to sell more than a few tickets for that performance. Only after Houdini had finally made his appearance did his stubborn admirers leave.

Reports of the skilfully-managed revolt spread all over England, and managers thereafter were far more cautious about attempting such sharp and unfair money-saving schemes.

But teaching caution to theater managers and learning to be cautious himself were two different things. Bessie was constantly worried about Houdini's well-being: he refused to let up for a single day, to rest for so much as an hour. He always contended that his body was in perfect condition, that it was part of his business to keep it that way, and that to worry about him was feminine and fruitless. He persisted in this attitude even when certain specific events occurred which would have persuaded a more temperate man to take some precautions.

He developed an abscess from his recurring struggles with strait jackets, and an operation was finally necessary. The surgery was not serious in itself, but it should have served as a warning to Houdini. Of course he refused to see it as such —and he also refused to heed the warning of a later, more serious, occurrence. He had been experiencing severe pain for some time, but refused to accept medical care until—during a performance in Pittsburgh, in the course of an American tour—he was finally forced to seek a doctor's help. The physician told him that one of his kidneys had been injured by some of his more strenuous escape routines. Houdini laughed at the medical orders of complete rest, finished his Pittsburgh engagement, and then finally paid token submission to the prescription by vacationing in New York for a brief two weeks. Afterward he played out the 1911-1912 season with his usual vigor, refusing to admit that he was in intense pain much of the time.

The summer of 1912 saw him the toast of New York and the star of Oscar Hammerstein's New Victoria Roof Garden. The always-wary New York press had succumbed completely to Houdini, and the Hammerstein engagement was held over time and time again. Houdini, still remembering his boyhood dream, demanded his salary in gold one day, and dramatically showered the glittering coins into his mother's lap. Mrs. Weiss glowed with pride and joy—but she was scarcely more enthusiastic than the American public.

The following year, in the midst of one more European tour, Houdini agreed to return to New York for a brief two-week engagement, to mark the opening of Hammerstein's for another season. His audience was ecstatic, following his "entrances and exits as breath-batedly as though he were really pushing himself through the small and hindermost entrance of a Yale lock," the New York *Sun* reported. "And," it added, "he would get out of there—that's the wonder of the man."

Houdini simply had no time to be ill or to take care of himself. But in Denmark, not long after his triumph at Hammerstein's in 1913, he received a delayed cable telling him that his mother had suffered a stroke. For the first time in his life Houdini broke a contract. He left for home immediately. But his mother died before he reached her.

And thereafter Houdini was, if not a more subdued person, certainly a changed man in many respects. His deep devotion to his mother had been one of the prime motivating forces of his life. Without it he was, for a long period, lost and heartsick. Her death affected him far more seriously than any injury to his own person could have done.

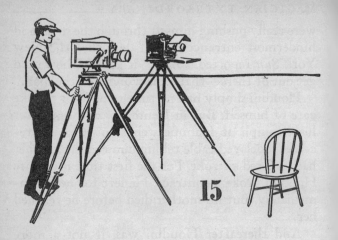

15

It was generally agreed by those who knew him best that his mother's death marked a turning point in Houdini's life. Afterward his enthusiasms—at least for a time—seemed less violent, his interest in life and work less strong. He delayed returning to his European tour, and when he did return, soon made plans for a month's vacation—the first such vacation he had ever taken. He also began to show a marked curiosity about spiritualism—not the fake "spirit shows" in which he had once indulged himself, but those apparently earnest and sincere efforts of people who truly believed they could communicate with the spirits of the dead. It was a curiosity which was to grow until it absorbed him entirely.

But before that occurred he did, slowly, pick up again the pieces of his life as one of the world's foremost entertainers. By the spring of 1914 he was touring England and Scotland with an act which, largely new, depended chiefly upon orthodox magic and illusions. One of his most dramatic effects was the so-called Needle Trick, which he had done for years, but only now began to feature.

Houdini had not invented it, but he did transform it from a "small" trick, suitable only for presentation to a few people, to one usable in a large hall. The trick is still available at magic supply houses today. Houdini's version of it showed him apparently swallowing several dozen needles and yards of thread, after which his assistants would draw out of his mouth the full

length of thread, with the needles now threaded
upon it. Eventually, when he was presenting th
stunt on the gigantic stage of the big old New
York Hippodrome, the thread was more than ;
hundred feet in length, stretching from one wing
to the other. It was an impressive and rathe
frightening performance, and Houdini astutely
capitalized on its seeming danger by inviting a
least one doctor to serve on the usual audience
inspection committee; none of them could eve
discover where Houdini concealed his threaded
needles. Did he indeed swallow them? The puzzle
brought people back to watch the performance
time after time.

Another illusion, this one with an interesting
escape twist, became a favorite topic of conversation throughout New York. The stunt was presented during one of the season-opening contracts
that Houdini was now regularly signing with
Hammerstein's summer Roof Garden. Houdini
had learned how to walk through a brick wall.

It was a singularly effective trick: on the stage,
in full view of the audience, a solid brick wall
would be constructed—often by volunteer teams
of union masons. The wall stood on a narrow
steel platform raised on casters for mobility; but
the casters lifted it only two or three inches off
the floor, and the audience realized that not even
a man of Houdini's flexibility could squeeze
through that narrow opening. When the wall was
194

completed—it was ordinarily built on one side of the stage, while the rest of the act proceeded in the middle—it was rolled forward and stood endwise to the audience. Before the wall was put in place, however, a committee from the audience was invited to inspect the rug covering the center portion of the floor, and the committee members always agreed that it had no openings of any kind. In order further to assure them, Houdini asked them to inspect a huge piece of white muslin, also innocent of any openings, which was thereafter laid over the rug.

Then, when the wall was in place, screens were set up on either side of it, to form small three-walled cabinets against the bricks. The committee was asked to stand around the entire wall, on the edge of the rug, to guard against Houdini's slipping around the far end of the wall. When everything was ready Houdini would step inside the screen on the right side, lift his arm above it in proof that he was actually there, lower his arm—and almost immediately it would appear on the other side. Whereupon the left screen would be moved, to reveal a Houdini none the worse for having apparently forced his body through solid brick. The incredulous committee would then again inspect the wall, the screens, and the muslin sheet—but they were in exactly the same condition as before. People marveled and questioned,

They saw Houdini "vanish" the biggest animal in the world.

and urged their friends to go immediately to witness the amazing performance.

One more of Houdini's illusions must also be mentioned here: the famous vanishing elephant. On the huge stage of the New York Hippodrome, Houdini waved a wand—and a huge pachyderm apparently dissolved into thin air. Other magicians might make rabbits disappear; Houdini, characteristically, proved that he could "vanish" —in the profession's phrase—the largest creature of them all.

An enormous cabinet on wheels would be rolled onto the stage; its double doors opened; and a committee's inspection invited. It was apparently solid. Then the elephant would be brought in, urged up a ramp into the cabinet, its doors would be closed for a brief moment, opened again—and the elephant would be gone. Where? Not through the stage floor, the audience knew: they could see between the cabinet's wheels; and in any case the Hippodrome stage was merely a wooden platform over the great water-filled tank utilized by its popular swimming performers. An elephant could not be lowered into a tank and expected to swim to safety. Where then *had* the elephant gone? The problem puzzled audiences for years—even today it puzzles many who still remember with awe that they saw Houdini vanish the biggest animal in the world.

The illusions had one advantage over Houdini's

escapes: they were not physically demanding. But as he regained his sense of vigor he persisted—despite frequent advice to the contrary—in performing stunts as arduous as any he had ever done in the past. He was still being strapped into strait jackets—and these were challenge jackets, furnished by local mental hospitals and departments of police—and hung head down from tall buildings. He was still doing his under-water escapes—although not quite so frequently, because they had become a markedly popular part of Hardeen's routine. (The brothers were still rivals in the public eye—a fact which they found highly amusing on the rare occasions when they were billed at competing theaters in the same town, and could meet late at night to compare notes and share family reminiscences.) And Houdini was now doing a new stunt which was surely as difficult as anything he had before attempted.

It was a development of the milk-can escape. The first change Houdini rang on that particular routine was to have the milk can sealed in a padlocked box, after he had been shut inside it. Then seeking an even more spectacular version he worked out what came to be known as the Chinese water-torture cell. The "cell" consisted of a heavy glass box, constructed on a metal frame, the lid of which was fitted with a pair of the stocks once used in New England to confine offenders of the peace. Houdini's feet would be put through the stocks, and then the lid would be placed on the water-filled box, so that Houdini was lowered head-first into the water. Padlocks sealed the box shut. There would be a final glimpse of Houdini, his water-distorted face near the box floor, before the curtains of the cabinet would be drawn and the orchestra began to play.

Audiences had found it grueling enough to *know* that Houdini had been submerged in water, and closed in a sturdy container; they found it even more compelling when they could actually *see* him in his glass-walled prison, apparently bound beyond the possibility of escape and condemned to death by drowning. Their cheers when he reappeared, drenched but triumphant, had the shrill sound of near-hysterical relief.

No, Houdini was not sparing himself. During the years of the First World War he toured back and forth across the United States, appearing at army camps and bond rallies as well as on his own crowded schedule of shows. His popularity made him a great drawing card at charitable and patriotic events, and Houdini was always willing to give his time and his talents—provided only that no prankish master of ceremonies attempted to introduce his turn with humorous comments. Laughter was as sternly excluded from his performance—and sometimes, it seemed, from his temperament—as it had ever been. He was admired for his courage and his skill. And sometimes that courage took other than physical forms.

One evening in Los Angeles, during the early war period, Houdini had reached that moment in his performance when he invited a committee to volunteer from the audience. Several persons had already offered themselves when Houdini, stepping forward, told the audience that he had noticed Jess Willard—then heavyweight champion of the world—seated in a box. The audience broke into cheers, and Houdini invited Willard to serve with the volunteers.

But the burly fighter—moved by an impulse he never afterward explained—chose to regard the invitation as an insult. "Go on with the show!" he growled.

Houdini, convinced that he had not made himself clear, repeated his request, and the audience seconded it with applause.

"If you pay me what you pay those seven men who are already on the stage, I'll come down," Willard called.

Houdini's volcanic temper exploded. He might perhaps have accepted a polite refusal to join the committee's ranks, though he would have been hurt. But Willard had done more than that; he had implied that Houdini *paid* those very volunteers whose purpose was to guarantee the integrity of his performance.

White-faced and furious, Houdini stepped

close to the box where the glowering champion sat. "I accept your challenge!" he declared. "Come right down—and I'll pay you exactly what I pay these seven men."

It is probably no exaggeration to say that he was taking both his life and his popularity in his hands. Willard, angry, could without doubt have done Houdini serious bodily injury. And Willard's worshipful following, equally angry, could have harmed Houdini's reputation forever. But into that tense moment after his bold words burst sudden applause. And the approval was for Houdini. The champion had offended by lack of sportsmanship.

Until then merely disagreeable and surly, Willard became suddenly a pillar of rage. "Go on with the show, you faker—you fourflusher!" he shouted. "Everyone knows you're a fourflusher!"

For the next quarter of an hour the theater was in an uproar. Houdini shouted back at Willard, and Willard answered more angrily than ever. The audience of some two thousand stamped and screamed and leaped up on their seats. Some were wildly applauding Houdini, others were as wildly hissing Willard. No one, it appeared, was willing to accept even a heavyweight champion's adverse verdict on the Escape King. Willard was finally compelled to leave the theater. The next day's papers contained innumerable sly references to the "new champion" who had defeated th titleholder.

It was a remarkable triumph for Houdini. H· had been in the public eye for a long time now and yet his audience was as staunch as it had beer a decade and a half earlier. This fact, togethei with the realization that he could not remain tc perform for them forever—his mother's death was a constant reminder of that—prompted hin to turn his attention, just after the war years, tc a new field of entertainment that was already growing rapidly: the world of the motion pic- ture. Perhaps there were other determining fac- tors as well. The movies were, even in those days, promising huge financial returns—and Houdini had not yet provided any security for his ad- vancing years. He was still spending money as rapidly as he made it, on lavish equipment and to further expand his enormous collections of magic books and materials. And, too, it was undoubted- ly a challenge to him to discover whether he might not add yet another crown to his head— whether he might not join Douglas Fairbanks and the few others then comprising the world's newest favorites, its motion picture stars.

Houdini's decision to appear in films was warmly welcomed in the trade. He could bring to the new industry a famous name, an enthusi- astic public, and a talent for thrilling escapes which ought—producers believed—to be well-adapted to the medium of motion pictures. Apparently it occurred to no one, least of all to Houdini, that acting ability might also be a requirement for success. In 1919 he made his first picture, a serial called "The Master Mystery," which was followed by two others, "The Grim Game" and "Terror Island." All utilized Houdini's best-known skills to the utmost: the stories were so devised that he was called upon to escape —and rescue the heroine—from every conceivable type of restraint, to slide down cliffs, to leap from one airplane to another in mid-air, to fight under water, and—of course—inevitably to defeat the villain. Houdini actually performed all the stunts shown on the screen, and he was injured more than once during the course of his work.

Unfortunately for him, however, many movie heroes were performing on the screen stunts which looked quite as dangerous as Houdini's— clever photography had already been widely accepted as an adequate substitute for courage. All of them could be made to *appear* to leap from one plane to another, although they may never have been more than a foot or two off the ground. And many of their performances were doubly effective because they were given by gifted actors, men able to imbue their scenes with reality, to portray tenderness and passion as well as extraordinary skill and strength.

It was only the last of those qualities that Houdini brought to his screen performances. He regarded the always-present heroine as a waste of screen footage, and his necessary scenes with her as useless interludes between stirring episodes of escape. The inevitable result was that the public, despite its admiration for Houdini's stage performances, refused to admire him as a screen hero. He wasn't, in the movies' own phrase, "the type."

Houdini, naturally enough, found it difficult to accept this startling judgment. And when he toured England, in 1920, and learned that his films were being fairly well received there—and had, indeed, served to introduce him to a whole new generation too young to have seen Houdini's prewar tour—he decided that the failure of his films in America had resulted from poor writing, direction, and production.

He had, of course, purchased a motion picture camera of his own, and was rapidly familiarizing himself with its techniques. He photographed his bridge-jumping stunts, his box escapes, his visits to the homes or graves of once-famous magicians —anything, in short, that he felt worthy of perpetuation. And soon he was opening his vaudeville performance with a series of these fragmentary bits of action, supplying the commentary himself as the scenes were flashed on the screen.

By the time he returned to the United States, in 1921, he was ready to form the Houdini Picture Corporation. He persuaded Hardeen to give up his own show to assume the less interesting business details, but he himself served as writer, director, editor, producer, and star. The new corporation made two pictures, "The Man from Beyond" and "Haldane of the Secret Service." The first was poorly received—even when Houdini made a personal appearance at the theater in an effort to convince a reluctant audience of the film's worth. The second was an utter failure. The venture was over almost before it had begun—although not until Houdini and the other investors had lost a considerable amount of money.

Houdini was nearing fifty, and his career seemed suddenly and inevitably to be nearing its end.

16

Many of Houdini's rivals had long looked forward to the day when the Great Houdini himself would assume the pitiful role of the has-been. Now at long last, they thought, that day was approaching.

But those rivals were disappointed. Houdini was, in fact, on the verge of one of the most spectacular periods of his career. He was about to become known to a larger audience than ever before, to win bigger and blacker headlines than in the past. Houdini as the world-famous campaigner against fraudulent mediums and spiritualists was about to come into being.

People wondered at the time—they still wonder today—whether his emergence in this striking new role was chiefly the result of a deep conviction, or merely another example of his superb showmanship. Probably the truth lay somewhere in between. Houdini couldn't stifle his showmanship, and never attempted to conceal the effort he put into the task of constantly rewinning a fickle public.

"No one except myself can appreciate how I

have to work at this job every single day, never letting up for a moment," he once wrote. "I always have on my mind the thought that next year I must do something greater, something more wonderful." His brilliant and highly publicized triumphs over spiritualists seemed indeed "greater" and "more wonderful" than many of his previous successes.

But there was at least a certain amount of conviction and honest anger behind his crusade. Houdini had known many "mediums" as fellow-performers, and had served as a "medium" in his youth. He knew only too well how most of their effects could be produced, and assumed that any he did not immediately understand could be penetrated by careful study. His instinctive reaction, when he saw a medium produce some new manifestation of voices or visible "spirits," was that of a well-informed magician: "It's a trick I never saw before. I must try to figure it out."

As he saw it, the magician and his public waged a constant battle of wits: the magician won the battle if he mystified his audience, by misdirection and skill and complete secrecy. (Houdini had his assistants all swear before a notary that they would never reveal the mechanisms of his escapes. Nearly a quarter of a century after his death one of those assistants, Lewis Goldstein, still refused to tell what he knew of how certain of Houdini's tricks were done.)

From this point of view it seemed to Houdini that the magician who called himself a medium—who spoke to the dead, produced ghosts, foretold the future—was violating a code. The medium warned his audience, in effect, "To understand is beyond your power—this is sacred. Do not try to understand: just believe." It seemed, to the adult Houdini, particularly despicable thus to take advantage of what he called "the hallowed reverence which the average human being bestows on the departed." He publicly admitted his shame for having himself ever "trifled" with that "reverence."

But he came to hope that there might be another side to the picture—that all mediums might not be deliberate tricksters. His mother's death had changed his attitude. His attachment to her had been so deep that he could not accept the fact that anything—even death—could separate them. For the first time in his life he wanted, genuinely and deeply, to believe that one could communicate with the world beyond the grave.

From 1913 on, then, he had been investigating whatever mediums crossed his path. He attended séances wherever he happened to be, read exhaustively in the field, and added many books on psychic research to his collection. With "an open mind devoutly anxious to learn if intercommunication is within the range of possibilities," he patiently visited mediums abroad and in this country.

The pattern of the séance seldom varied. The audience—the "seekers"—sat in a circle around a table, each holding the hand of the person on either side. The room would be darkened—"spirits" were said to find light a hostile element. Sometimes the "medium" would simply be part of the circle; sometimes he—or she—would be bound to a chair or locked into a cabinet as "evidence" that any manifestations that might take place could not be contrived by him. When all was ready and quiet, the medium would inquire whether any spirit was present and wished to speak. Sometimes there would be no response at all, and this was often attributed to the fact that there was some unfriendly person in the room, someone whose lack of faith prevented the spirit from "getting through."

But sometimes the answer would come. If the medium was under the "control" of a single spirit with whom he regularly communicated, the controlling spirit might relay messages from other spirits, stating that "Henry says to tell Mrs. Smith not to sell the house," or "Ellen sends love to her mother and tells her she is happy." Or the invited spirits might appear individually, making their presence known by voices or other signs. These latter might be signals tapped out on a table, notes rung on a bell, or messages written on the inner side of two sealed slates. There might, of course, also be visual manifestations—objects floating through the air, or the sudden appearance, usually from the medium's mouth, of a pale phosphorescent "spirit substance" called ectoplasm.

Other people might be impressed because they could not explain what they had seen or heard. But "many things that seem wonderful to most men are the everyday commonplaces of my business," Houdini wrote.

On one memorable occasion, in 1914 when he was aboard a transatlantic liner with Theodore Roosevelt, he astounded "Teddy"—and subsequently the world, through excited stories in the press—by a performance of which many self-proclaimed mediums would have been proud. At an impromptu séance Houdini had offered to answer questions put by the guests. The questions

were written on slips of paper that were then sealed between two slates. The answers subsequently appeared written on the inner surface of one of the slates.

Roosevelt, chuckling over his own query, which he confidently believed would stump even Houdini's ingenuity, carefully superintended the sealing of the slates, and then awaited Houdini's admission of failure. His question was: "Where did I spend Christmas?" But to his amazement, when the slates were opened, one was found to be covered with an elaborate map of the part of South America which "Teddy" had recently been exploring; his route was accurately marked out; and a cross indicated the very spot where he had in truth been camping on Christmas day. Houdini's feat seemed particularly incredible because the details of Roosevelt's trip had not yet been made public.

Actually the trick—for it had of course been a trick—was merely another example of Houdini's willingness to expend considerable time and energy in order to achieve a desired effect. Before he boarded the ship he had learned that Roosevelt would be a fellow-passenger. He had not needed to foretell the future to know that he would be asked to present a show of some sort during the voyage—he was always asked to do so and never refused. If, this time, he were not invited to produce "psychic" phenomena, he could easily enough persuade some suggestible passenger to make just that proposal. Houdini had become a master at insinuating ideas into other people's minds—ideas which they later offered quite innocently as their own.

With businesslike purpose, then, he visited a friendly newspaperman before he sailed, copied the detailed map which the paper was holding for future publication, read the account of Roosevelt's travels, prepared his slate—and then made ready several slips of paper that he intended to "plant" among the passengers' questions. Each of the slips read "Where did Roosevelt spend Christmas?" But shortly before the séance was to take place he made one more preparation. He casually distributed about on the various tables of the ship's lounge several books that he "fixed" by slitting the cover, inserting a piece of paper and a carbon, and resealing the binding again. While the passengers were writing their questions Houdini graciously offered Roosevelt a book to use as a support, and Roosevelt accepted.

A moment later Houdini had retrieved the book and read the message. He was startled and delighted to find the very question for which he had prepared an answer, and swiftly discarded his own "planted" slips. Thereafter everything was easy. In Houdini's own words, "I did not have to resort to sleight of hand, but boldly asked him to place his question between the slates himself, as I held them in the air. While I pretended to show all four faces of the two slates, by manipulation I showed only three. My 'message' . . . was already on one slate as I tied the two of them face together. . . . It can be readily seen why the Colonel was willing to believe that I possessed the power of drawing communications from spirits, whereas I was simply resorting to a material experiment, in which, as it turned out, blind chance played a large part."

But were there those who did in fact possess that "power of drawing communications from spirits"? Houdini sincerely desired to know. In 1920, in England, he had met Sir Arthur Conan Doyle, and learned that there was at least one highly intelligent man who believed so.

Their meeting was a curious and stimulating experience for both men. Sir Arthur, who had only recently been converted to a belief in spiritualism, was so convinced of its value and importance to the world that he had abandoned *Sherlock Holmes* and all his other writings to preach what was to him a new religion. He found Houdini's knowledge of spiritualism as wide as his own; but their attitudes toward it were entirely different. Houdini's "everyday commonplaces" all seemed "wonderful" to Sir Arthur, and although—like Houdini—he was eager to expose fraudulent mediums, he was less able to see how fraud might be accomplished.

Houdini told him much of what he himself knew about the tricks of the trade, and Doyle was both interested and grateful. But he, in turn, explained to Houdini that many of the mediums he knew were, he was sure, honest people incapable of fraud. He pointed out that Houdini's explanations for allegedly "psychic" phenomena might be correct—but that, again, they might not. Was it not possible, Sir Arthur asked, that writing on a slate *might* have been produced by a spirit hand? The fact that Houdini knew it *could* have been produced otherwise, was no proof that it had indeed always happened as he suggested.

Their arguments were long and inconclusive. Neither was convinced of anything he had not believed before. But Houdini's interest in the whole field had been increased by their talks.

Even during the busy year of 1920-21, when he was engaged in the making of his last two motion pictures, he still found time to visit spiritualists and maintain his steady purchase of books on the subject. During the latter part of 1921, while he was making a brief Keith tour of the United States, he sought out mediums in every town he visited. And when, during that same year, his book, *Miracle Mongers and Their Methods*, was published—it was a historical account of fire-eaters, sword swallowers, strong men and other "freaks" so well-known to Houdini from his dime museum days—he decided that his next volume would be devoted to the spiritualists and *their* methods—or, at least, their methods as Houdini understood them.

His personal interest was expanding; his private search transforming itself into a typically publicized program.

Two factors may have hastened that development. Both concerned Sir Arthur Conan Doyle.

Early in 1922 Doyle and his wife were in this country on a lecture tour in behalf of spiritualism, and the Houdinis visited them for a few days at their Atlantic City hotel. Lady Doyle, who did "automatic writing," offered to try to obtain for Houdini a message from his mother, and the magician eagerly—and apparently hopefully—agreed. He and the Doyles went alone into a quiet room, and after a few moments of prayer Lady Doyle was, as Houdini later described it, " 'seized by a Spirit'. . . . Her hand beat on the table, her whole body shook, and at last, making a cross at the head of the page, she started writing."

Doyle always claimed that Houdini was deeply moved by the resulting message, beginning, "Oh, my darling, thank God, thank God, at last I'm through," and stating that soon Houdini would "get all the evidence he is so anxious for." Houdini himself insisted that he had never for a moment been convinced that the words had been dictated by his mother's spirit. The date of the "writing" was the anniversary of his mother's birthday, and he believed that if it had indeed been she speaking to him, that fact, and Houdini's religious observance of the anniversary, would have been mentioned; furthermore, he pointed out, the message had been in English, a language never used between Mrs. Weiss and her son. Doyle protested that neither language nor earthly dates had any significance to a spirit, but Houdini refused to be persuaded. He did not think the Doyles had deliberately deceived him; he thought, rather, that they were themselves deceived by their naïve credulity.

The cleavage between the two men, which probably began with that event, was deepened by a curious circumstance that may also have influenced Houdini's attitude: Doyle became convinced that Houdini himself was a medium, capable of more-than-human behavior. He declared that Houdini could perform certain of his tricks only by "dematerializing"—that is, dissolving his physical body—and "rematerializing" it later.

Houdini's consistent reply to such statements was the flat declaration that he accomplished all his escapes and other feats by purely physical means—but he decided that it was his duty to protect the public from those who preached as Doyle did. He stated—and often repeated—that he maintained an open mind; that he did not assume, prior to investigation, that all mediums and spiritualists were frauds. And in substantiation of this claim he made many pacts with those men he knew best, whereby each promised that, if he were to die first, he would make every attempt to communicate with the other by means of a secret code. None of those pacts produced messages which Houdini accepted as genuine; but their existence proved, he said, that he *wished* to believe.

His increasing efforts to expose mediums, however, soon convinced all spiritualists that Houdini was one of the principal enemies of their creed. They objected strenuously to the "spook" lectures which he began to give during a personal-appearance tour with his movies in 1922. And, early in 1923, when Houdini became a member of the Committee for Psychical Investigation organized by the *Scientific American Magazine*, all spiritualists felt that Houdini had officially joined himself with the opposing forces.

Certainly, whatever Houdini's personal attitude from that time on, his public performance formed the spearhead of attacks on the spiritualist belief.

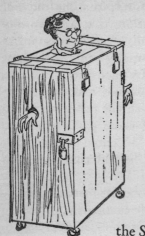

17

Programs like the one the *Scientific American* organized were not, of course, new. And the $2,500 award the magazine offered to any medium who could prove to the satisfaction of its investigating committee that he—or she—possessed genuine psychic powers, was merely another in a series of such awards. The British Society for Psychical Research had been founded some time earlier, and its activities were almost as well known as those of some of the more famous spiritualists, such as the Davenport Brothers and D. D. Home. The latter thrilled royalty by his "levitation" (his body was lifted into the air without visible means of support and —according to report—floated at will near the ceiling, or drifted nonchalantly in and out of second-story windows). Houdini's boyhood friend, J. H. Rinn, with whom Houdini had practised "spiritualist's" rope ties, had become one of the most active of the exposers in the United States and was one of those who urged Houdini to add his talents to the task.

Houdini was the only magician on the *Scientific American's* committee. He was not always co-operative—he was arrogant about having his own way, and inclined to feel that he alone of the group was capable of judging a medium's merits—but the renown he brought to the program was compensation enough.

A young Italian named Nino Pecararo was prominent among the early entries for the award. Houdini doubted the young man's honesty—even before he saw him perform—when he learned from his fellow-committeemen that in preparation for his séance Pecararo permitted himself to be tied with sixty feet of rope.

"Sixty feet!" Houdini repeated scornfully— and proceeded to give the committee a lecture on rope ties, pointing out that even an inexperienced man could get his hands free when he had the inevitable slack such a length provided.

At Houdini's suggestion the young man was thereupon tied with several short ropes. Although the subsequent séance lasted for nearly an hour and a half, no ghosts appeared, and no spirit voices were heard. Pecararo's reputation as a medium was shattered.

Houdini thereafter took part in many other investigations, including that of the young Spaniard named Argamasilla, who came to the United States heralded by the enthusiastic acclaim of many European scientists. Argamasilla claimed to have what he called "X-ray vision," enabling him to see through metal: he could tell time by a watch whose face was concealed by its closed metal case, and could answer questions which he "read" through the metal top of the box into which they had been locked.

Houdini made short work of Argamasilla. He watched the husky young man blindfold himself, pick up a watch—whose hands had been set a moment before by an investigator, and its cover snugly shut—hold the watch at shoulder height, lower it, lift it high again, and then announce the exact minute which the hands indicated. Houdini knew instantly that as Argamasilla brought his hand down he opened the watch cover slightly, and that he could read the face by looking down along his cheeks under the blindfold. Houdini thereupon offered him a watch which was difficult to open—and Argamasilla failed in his test.

Argamasilla's gold and silver boxes were no greater problem to the magician. Houdini realized that their construction permitted their lids to be lifted a fraction of an inch, and the slip of paper inside thus read through the narrow opening. The "X-ray vision" king refused to perform when Houdini offered two boxes of his own preparation. Like Pecararo, the Spaniard was discredited.

The great case, however, was that of the famous Margery who proved to be a more powerful adversary. Wife of the Boston surgeon, Dr. L. R. G. Crandon, she was a woman of unusual intelligence and a highly respected member of her community. Deliberate fraud seemed alien to her nature. By the time the committee initiated its official investigation of her powers, she had a large and devoted following—and many of those followers never deserted her. At least one member of the committee itself had, in fact, publicly declared, prior to the investigation, that the *Scientific American*'s award had probably found its claimant.

Houdini entered this particular investigation somewhat belatedly—he blamed the committee's secretary for not having called him in earlier—and his resultant anger added aggressiveness to his usual suspicion. He was immediately convinced that Margery's séances—held around a table in a darkened room—were actually accomplished by ordinary conjuring; that the spirit voices, bell-ringing, and other usual manifestations—produced, according to the medium, by the "controlling" spirit of her dead brother, Walter—were not psychic phenomena. He believed, for example, that she rang the electric bell with her foot. But he found proof of his quick conviction somewhat difficult to establish.

"Anticipating the sort of work I would have to do in detecting the movements of her foot," Houdini wrote later, "I had rolled my right trouser leg up above my knee. All that day I had worn a silk rubber bandage around that leg just below the knee. By night the part of the leg below the bandage had become swollen and painfully tender, thus giving me a much keener sense of feeling and making it easier to notice the slightest sliding of Mrs. Crandon's ankle or flexing of her muscles. . . . As the séance progressed I could distinctly feel her ankle slowly and spasmodically sliding as it pressed against mine while she gained space to raise her foot off the floor and touch the top of the box. . . . When she had finally maneuvered her foot around to a point where she could get at the top of the box, the bell ringing began and *I positively felt* the tendons of her leg flex and tighten as she repeatedly touched the ringing apparatus. There is no question in my mind about it. *She did this.* Then, when the ringing was over, I plainly *felt her leg slide back* into its original position with her foot on the floor beside mine."

Houdini was similarly certain that when the table was overthrown "by Walter," it had actually been Margery herself who accomplished it by bending down and thrusting her head beneath the edge. *"I caught her doing this twice,"* he wrote in emphatic italics.

But once the lights were on again, it was his word against Margery's as to what had gone on in the dark. And the other members of the committee, unlike Houdini, had a certain diffidence about calling the lady a liar. It was finally agreed that Houdini should construct a foolproof cabinet in which Margery would sit for their next session. The cabinet would allow only her head and hands to protrude, and the hands would, as usual, be held by the persons sitting on either side of her.

The first séance held with the cabinet—a kind of upright wooden coffin—was successful, from Margery's point of view. The bell, placed on a table before her, rang. Houdini was convinced that she had opened the top of the cabinet and stretched forward far enough to touch the bell with her head. At the subsequent trial the cabinet was therefore sealed "with four hasps, staples, and padlocks," and that time her hands were also shut inside. That time the bell did not ring.

But Houdini's triumph was not complete. "Walter's" loud angry voice broke the silence: "Houdini, you are very clever indeed, but it won't work. You left a rule in the cabinet—you blackguard! You are trying to throw suspicion on my sister. Get out of here, Houdini, and never come back!"

Houdini, convinced that the voice was actually Margery's, wrote, "This just expressed Mrs. Crandon's feelings toward me, for she knew I had her trapped." He was also convinced that the two-foot wooden rule—which was indeed found in the cabinet when it was opened—had been smuggled in by Mrs. Crandon herself, with the hope that she could manipulate it with her head sufficiently to ring the bell. Mrs. Crandon, on the other hand—as "Walter" had suggested—accused Houdini of having "planted" the rule to discredit her.

The matter was never settled to everyone's satisfaction. Margery was not given the magazine's award in token of genuine mediumship, but she nevertheless remained triumphant in the eyes of many, among whom was Conan Doyle.

The earlier friendship between the two men had by then come to an unhappy end. ". . . you force me to speak," Doyle had written Houdini, "and I have no wish to offend you. But you can't have it both ways. You can't bitterly and offensively—often also untruly—attack a subject and yet expect courtesies from those who honor that subject. It is not reasonable."

Houdini was regretful but adamant. One incident, reported by Houdini's lawyer, Bernard Ernst, in his book, *Houdini and Conan Doyle*, suggests that Houdini's pride in his own ability

rather than any earnest desire to convince Doyle
of error, lay at the bottom of his attitude.

Ernst and Doyle were at Houdini's home one
evening—before the author and the magician
had ceased to meet on friendly terms—and Houdini presented an illusion which he said he had
worked out for their special entertainment. His
materials consisted of a large slate with small
holes in the two upper corners, two pieces of wire,
four small round balls, a bottle of white ink, and
a spoon.

At Houdini's request Doyle himself tied the
two wires through the holes in the slate and hung
it up in such a way that it swung free in the
center of the room. Then the two guests were
asked to inspect the four balls, and to cut one
open to assure themselves that they were—as
Houdini said—spheres of solid cork. The three
remaining balls were then dropped into the bottle
of white ink.

The stage was set. Houdini next asked Sir Arthur to leave the house—to leave the city, if he
chose—and, in secret, write some brief message
on a slip of paper which he would thereafter hide
on his person and show to no one. Doyle agreed,
walked three blocks from the Houdini house,
turned a corner, and confident that he was not
being seen, wrote "Mene, mene, tekel upharsin"
on the slip that he then folded and hid in an
inner pocket. When he returned to the house

Ernst assured him that Houdini himself had not so much as left the room during his absence.

Slowly Houdini lifted one small cork ball out of the ink, with the spoon he had provided. He held the ball and spoon against the slate—and removed the spoon. The ball mysteriously remained adhered to the slate. It was still for a moment, then began to roll aimlessly over the black surface, leaving a track of white in its wake. Finally it began to write. The words it formed were "Mene, mene, tekel upharsin"!

The discussion that followed was heated. Doyle was certain that Houdini had undeniably exhibited psychic powers. Houdini insisted that he had merely performed a trick—a difficult trick, and one demanding considerable preparation, but nevertheless a trick.

"Well, Houdini," Ernst said finally, "you could settle the matter very definitely, one way or the other, by disclosing either to Sir Arthur or to me, just how the feat was accomplished."

"This, however, Houdini refused to do," Ernst wrote afterward, "and there the matter rested. What is one to think of this extraordinary occurrence? . . . Houdini was constantly doing things of this sort, and in his refusal to disclose the secret of his methods, must have been thoroughly tantalizing to those who were half-inclined to believe that what he did was really genuine, and that he merely refused to admit the fact. . . ."

To the spiritualists Houdini must indeed have been tantalizing and infuriating as well. To the general public he was, quite frankly, a hero. In early 1924 he made a brief lecture tour devoted exclusively to the subject of spiritualism. His biographer, Harold Kellock, who shortly after the magician's death wrote Houdini's life story with the aid of Bessie Houdini, points out that "he elected to tour the provinces in a series of one-night stands as a lecturer, at a lecturer's wage. Having won the position of prince of entertainers, some irresistible urge within him now made it impossible for him ever to be merely an entertainer again." But in one way the lecture tour made possible for Houdini what he might not otherwise have achieved: his continued hold on public attention.

It had become clear that he could not successfully attach himself—as many other performers were trying to do—to the new and rising motion picture world. And even his greatest admirers doubted that he could maintain for long an enormous popularity as a vaudevillian, when vaudeville itself was shrinking rapidly in the face of the movie's growth. But as a campaigner against spiritualism Houdini was entering a fairly new and almost empty field. He made the most of it —and his most was very good.

He followed that lecture tour by preparing and touring with an elaborate show in which he featured—together with some of the more popular items from his previous days—a séance presented in such a way that the audience could see exactly how the usual spiritualistic phenomena were accomplished. The tour opened with spectacular success at New York's Hippodrome.

Once more he utilized the technique of the volunteer committee, but now the committee members were hooded and seated around a table on the stage. Two of them held tightly—or so they believed—to Houdini's hands. The noises and other phenomena which then took place seemed to the committee members as inexplicable as such phenomena ordinarily did to the visitors at a darkened séance. The group always testified afterward that Houdini had not escaped their grasp, and that his feet had not moved. But the theater audience could watch, in the full light of the stage, how Houdini actually contrived his effects. They could see him slip his feet out of his shoes and use his toes to ring bells and shake a tambourine. They could see how an assistant under the table cleverly substituted the slates on which an unsuspecting committeeman had written a question, for other slates on which the committeeman subsequently found a "spirit" reply. Houdini used all of the most popular spiritualist phenomena, and exposed them all as he performed.

The audience loved it. Newspapers called Houdini's crusade a triumph of intelligence over superstition. The editorials praising him would have filled huge scrapbooks. "It was a sad day for the spiritualistic 'mediums' when they permitted Harry Houdini, the magician, to watch some of their demonstrations," the Providence *News* declared; "Houdini knows a few tricks himself and he knows them even better than the cleverest psychic frauds. . . . More power to Houdini to run the fakirs out of business."

The newspapers even co-operated in Houdini's performance by permitting him to obtain, each evening just before curtain time, the news being prepared for the next day's paper. Houdini would then report these apparently as-yet-unknown events from the stage—and promptly refute the possibility of clairvoyance by thereafter explaining how he knew that a fire had just broken out across town or that within the hour a revolution had started in some foreign country.

Showman and crusader worked happily hand in hand. Even the old challenge technique was still useful, in a new guise. All of Houdini's souvenir programs carried his personal "CHALLENGE TO ANY MEDIUM IN THE WORLD" to present "so-called 'psychical' manifestations that I cannot reproduce or explain as being accomplished by natural means." He offered to donate to charity "any sum up to $10,000" if his challenge were met—but although he sometimes flourished actual bills in the face of a spiritualist, the money was never paid out.

His fiftieth birthday came and went, and he noted in his diary that he could hardly believe it, that he did not feel his age "in body and far from it in mind." But when he published an account of the Margery and Argamasilla tests, he said he did so because "Dame Nature will eventually demand her toll" and he would not always be alive "to give a personal account of my connection with these séances."

In the meantime his book, *A Magician Among the Spirits*, had been issued, and it too added to the fires of controversy and fame. It was both a lively historical report and a highly personalized success-story dramatizing Houdini's encounters with the world of spiritualism. Nonspiritualists were inclined to call it definitive and scientifically accurate. Spiritualists accused Houdini of errors so flagrant as to be deliberate untruths. Ernst, evaluating the book years later, said that his friend and client had undoubtedly been "guilty of some historic blunders—names, dates, facts of all kinds being incorrectly given. It would be possible to fill several typewritten pages with these errors."

If Houdini had been alive when Ernst's statement was made, his reaction would have been particularly interesting. Houdini had once specifically derided Robert-Houdin for his "supreme egotism, his obvious desire to make all his autobiography picturesque and interesting rather than historically correct, and his utter indifference to dates, exact names of places, theaters, books, etc. . . ." It would seem that Houdini had lived to emulate his one-time hero more closely than he had perhaps intended. He, too, had become world-famous; he, too, had written books that were widely read—and he, too, had obvious failings that offered an easy handle to would-be detractors.

If the measure of a man's greatness is the number of his enemies, Houdini had certainly far outstripped the man for whom he had named himself. But part of his expert showmanship was the use he had learned to make of those enemies —the advantage he created out of everyone who disagreed with him, who quarreled with him, and with whom he quarreled.

The jealous rivals who had, time after time, predicted Houdini's end as a performer, now—when he had already held the public for the remarkable period of a quarter-century—now even those rivals admitted that he would probably never let it go so long as he lived.

18

In the spring of 1925—Houdini was fifty-one that April—he decided once more to organize and manage his own show for the following season. It did seem that this time he could hardly fail. Audiences all over the country were eager to join in the game he made of "spoofing the spooks," and the inevitable presence of a certain number of earnest spiritualists in each town provided a guarantee of conflict and drama.

Bessie and Ernst tried to persuade him to rest during the summer if he were really determined upon so rigorous a program, but Houdini had never known how to rest and he could not learn now. When he wasn't lecturing, he was managing a "raid" on a séance, working out a new trick, or refurbishing an old one. He was again stubbornly insisting that he would present, as window dressing for his main act, some of the "little magic" from his earlier days. He was out of practice at that time and needed considerable rehearsing. His correspondence was voluminous, his library and collections still demanded much of his time, and there was a great deal of work involved in directing the dozen agents whom he sent out ahead of his tour to visit spiritualists along the proposed route.

When the Houdini tour opened in the fall, it was clear from the start that even Houdini's lack of business acumen could not prevent its success. Every performance had its spectacular quality. Sometimes Houdini had previously posted in the lobby the names of the local mediums he intended to expose, sometimes he made the exposures without warning. In most cases the mediums themselves attended his shows, drawn by a curiosity greater than their fear. Houdini sometimes even made them unwilling participants in his performance.

His agents did their work well. They would arrive in a town in advance of the show, visit local mediums, and posing as believers, pay for and receive supposedly genuine messages from the spirit world. Some of these messages had, to the skeptical Houdini crew, a note of purest comedy. Time after time an unmarried agent would receive words of comfort or advice from the spirit of a "late husband" or a "lamented wife"; childless agents were constantly being assured by the spirits of their nonexistent offspring that "Mummy" or "Daddy" mustn't worry over their fate—that they were happy in Heaven.

With obvious relish Houdini would quote these remarkable messages from the platform. His denunciation would be followed by the focusing of a spotlight on the unfortunate medium seated in the audience. The startled flights of spiritualists from the audience, like birds fluttering wildly away from a menacing cat, were frequent occurrences—and were always good for enormous publicity. Houdini never failed to derive pleasure from the fact that one of his agents used the pseudonym "F. Raud," and that none of her victims was ever put on guard by the very combination of letters that had proved Kleppini's downfall when Houdini used them on the old letter cuff.

Back and forth across the country the triumphant Houdini tour made its way. Three metropolitan newspapers were publishing daily accounts, written by Houdini, of his exposures. In Philadelphia a near-riot ensued when Houdini challenged the "millionaire medium," John Slater, to read the sealed messages Houdini held in his hand—and Slater refused. The Chicago newspapers carried the flashlight photograph Houdini had made of a local medium at the very moment when a supposed "spirit" message was being delivered: the picture showed the medium herself with a megaphone against her lips. On another occasion Houdini flashed sudden lights on a medium whose hands and face were seen to be covered with lampblack—lampblack that Houdini had smeared on the "spirit's" megaphone before the séance started.

Of course the exposures resulted in suits against Houdini, in counterinvestigations, and countercharges of fraud. Houdini welcomed them all. He enjoyed appearing in court.

He especially enjoyed being asked to testify before the committees set up by the United States Senate and House of Representatives, when a resolution had been presented in Congress aimed at outlawing fraudulent mediums from Washington, D.C. The hearings were full of incident. Houdini regarded them as additional excuses for brilliant performances, and gave a demonstration séance that startled some of the lawmakers out of their seats. The resolution failed to pass, but the hearings resulted in the unofficial exposure of many of the capital's mediums. The accusations against Houdini which were called forth—challenging both his morality and his sanity—merely provided the magician with further opportunities for melodramatic speeches.

Almost anyone but Houdini would have rested content for months to come with the notoriety of those proceedings. But Houdini sprang directly into preparations for what has been called "probably the most difficult feat of his career." While Washington had been reading eagerly of Houdini's statements from the witness box, New York had been just as eagerly flocking to see a man who could—he claimed, and appeared to prove—suspend animation in his body for ten minutes or more. Doctors seemed unable to explain the physiology of the "trance" into which Rahmen Bey, as he called himself, could slip at will and from which he returned as from the dead. Thousands were insisting that in this man they had at last found positive evidence of supernatural powers.

It was the sort of claim Houdini could not let go unchallenged. Starting with the assumption that Rahmen Bey did not have such powers, Houdini determined to prove that he himself could better the man's feat by applying the merely human powers which, he insisted, limited both their accomplishments. As if unaware that he had already subjected his body to far more strain than the average man of his age could endure, he set himself an arduous program of under-water and slow-breathing practice.

Rahmen Bey performed in an airtight coffin on the stage of a theater. When Houdini was ready—in August of 1926—he announced that he, too, would be locked in such a coffin, and that

237

it would then be lowered under water—to counter any possibility of trickery. The test was made, before doctors and reporters, in the swimming pool of a New York hotel. Capable swimmers were enlisted to hold the coffin below the surface. The physicians present agreed that the oxygen in the coffin might last the average man for less than fifty breaths, but that Houdini might conceivably know how to use it so sparingly that he could exist without additional air for fifteen minutes.

Houdini made a speech before the coffin was shut, reiterating his claim that he would use nothing more than highly-practised skill. And then the lid was sealed and the huge box lowered into the pool.

The minutes ticked by until half an hour had passed. The doctors shook their heads. Houdini was not a fool—but he was a gray-haired man in his middle years, and he had no right, they thought, to put himself under such a strain. By the end of an hour several of them were insisting that, despite Houdini's orders, the coffin should be lifted and opened. But Houdini's own assistants refused—although Rahmen Bey's record had now been surpassed.

At the end of an hour and a half the tiled walls around the pool reverberated to nervous whispers. And when, a minute later, the signal for ascent was given, it was a group of very frightened men who hauled the coffin out of the water and hastily pried off its top. The doctors were seriously alarmed at the state of Houdini's blood pressure, respiration, and temperature. But while they were still using the words "extreme exhaustion," Houdini dressed and disappeared. He admitted to feeling tired, but he thought what he needed was an hour or so of exercise.

That fall he took his huge show out again, but he had promised Bessie that he would keep it on the road only one more year. After that, he explained, he would no longer have time for it; there were too many other things he had long wanted to do. Even to listen to him discuss his future plans was tiring to an ordinary man. His projects included, among other things, several more books, more lecturing, a possible University of Magic, and the development of at least one new trick which he someday meant to perfect (he intended to learn how to escape from a solid block of ice).

In September the show went well. Houdini's only problem was to fit all his varied interests into each day. But early the following month, in Providence, Bessie was seized with a severe attack of ptomaine poisoning. Houdini secured a nurse for her and then, worried and doubly burdened with all the details that Bessie usually attended to, dashed down to New York for business conferences. They kept him on his feet, with only a single hour's rest, for three days and nights, after which he hurried to Albany to do a show there. That night, while he was presenting the Chinese water-torture cell, a sharp spasm of pain warned him of danger. He had himself lifted out of the cell and discovered that his ankle was broken. But he went grimly through the rest of the performance, hopping on one foot. And for the next three days, against all medical advice, he played out his shows wearing a brace he had devised.

The brace also got him through the remainder of the week in Schenectady and the subsequent

week in Montreal. Friday afternoon of that week two students, who had heard him give a lecture a few days before at Montreal's McGill University, called upon Houdini in his dressing room. Houdini was courteous—one of the boys had made a sketch of the performer which delighted him—but so preoccupied with his mail that he paid little attention to their conversation. One of them asked a question about his ability to withstand blows, and he replied that he could do so if his muscles were braced in anticipation. The boy spoke again, and this time Houdini only murmured absent-mindedly, unaware of what had been said.

An instant later the boy leaned over the couch, where Houdini was lying to rest his still-unmended ankle, and struck him several times sharply in the abdomen with his clenched fist. At Houdini's startled gesture the boy stopped, backed away, and explained apologetically that he had asked if he might test Houdini's muscles —and that Houdini had agreed. The boy was stricken with remorse—Houdini was clearly in pain—but soon afterward the performer relieved his fears by stepping out on the stage for his afternoon show.

Late that night, however, Houdini admitted that he was suffering increasing discomfort. His performance the following day was two and a half hours of concentrated agony, except for those moments during the intermission when he fell into a stupefied doze. But he took his scheduled train that evening, to Detroit. The doctors summoned to meet him at the station in the morning diagnosed appendicitis and ordered an immediate operation, but Houdini insisted that he must appear in the theater that evening. When he walked out on the stage he had a temperature of 104°.

Even his fierce and dogged determination could not muster the strength he needed for his performance. Time after time, during the show, terrified assistants had to step forward to complete some motion which Houdini could not manage. He remained on the stage until the end, but he collapsed when the curtain was rung down.

An operation was performed immediately. The surgeons agreed that peritonitis was far advanced. They said Houdini would probably not live through the following day. Bessie was not told the truth—she was still ill herself and they feared its effect on her.

But it was seven days later—October 31, 1926 —when Houdini at last turned toward Bessie and his brother Hardeen, and said quietly, "I'm tired of fighting, Dash." He died shortly afterward.

The coffin in which he had bested Rahmen Bey's "supernatural" record was discovered to be among his equipment on the road, and it was in this that his body was shipped back to New York.

He was buried beside his mother in the family plot he had purchased years before in the Machpelah Cemetery, Cypress Hills. The Society of American Magicians, of which he had been Most Illustrious President for ten years, held a service in his honor.

Houdini had been a "story" until the last moment. Reporters had stood by during his gallant battle against death—a battle as remarkable as any he had ever waged against fraudulent mediums—to rush the physicians' twice-daily reports to their papers. And he continued to be a "story" after his death.

The controversy over whether the blow delivered by the student had actually been responsible for the rupturing of Houdini's appendix was finally settled—for the official record, at least—when Houdini's insurance policy was paid according to the double indemnity rate permissible in accidental death.

There was considerable excitement in theatrical circles when Hardeen, "brother of the Great Houdini," took up Houdini's tour where he had abandoned it, and carried on as Houdini's official successor.

It was news when the announcement appeared that Houdini's enormous library of magic and theatrical lore had been left to the Library of Congress.

But the public was particularly aware of the

furor Houdini's death caused among spiritualists. Conan Doyle repeated his belief in Houdini's mediumship, and shortly before his own death, a few years later, wrote to Ernst that he might be "talking it all over with Houdini himself before very long."

Many spiritualists who claimed the ability to read the future had "foretold" Houdini's death, and he had always laughed at them. He had pointed out that since he must die sometime, one of them was eventually bound to be right. He would probably have been equally amused at the numbers, after his death, who claimed to have received messages from his "spirit." But the fact that he himself had always retained some lingering hope in the possibility of communication was probably evident in the pact he had made with Bessie some time before: he had promised to communicate with her from the "other world" if it were at all possible. "And if anybody can get through, I should be able to," he had added, half seriously, half in skepticism.

Bessie Houdini held her private "séances" faithfully. It was not until years later, shortly before her death in 1943, that she gave them up. She had never received what she could accept as a genuine visitation of Houdini's spirit. Nor did she—although she was hopeful once or twice— feel that any of the eager spiritualists had ever received a message capable of passing the tests to which Houdini himself would have put it.

Today, of course, it is not so much the spiritualists who remember him best—although he still stands high in the list of those they regard as enemies for all time. Today he is better remembered by magicians who applaud his skill and still envy his spectacular showmanship, and by young people to whom he represents the very spirit of mystification—the delight all human beings take in amazing others and in being amazed themselves.

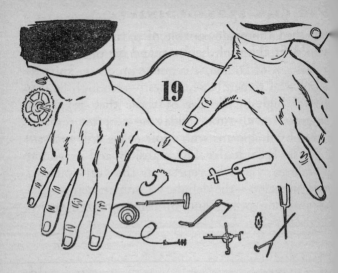

19

What were Houdini's secrets? How did he succeed in amazing others so completely and for so long a time?

The milk-can escape, for example, one of Houdini's most successful tricks, puzzled not only audiences but other magicians, and few attempted to imitate it. Even if they believed they had discovered its secret, they were unwilling to attempt the grueling under-water work it entailed.

It did have a secret, of course, like most of his other escapes: the neck of the can was detachable from the body, and Houdini could—by exerting great pressure—lift it up from the inside and step out. Then, without ever having

246

touched the padlocks fastening the lid down, he could fit the neck back on and have it instantly ready for the committee's investigation. The possibility of danger was always present, as it was in most of Houdini's tricks; in this case the danger was that the neck might become jammed. But, actually, Houdini's only close call with this stunt occurred the night a local brewer filled the can with beer. Houdini's inexperience with alcohol in any form made him particularly susceptible to its fumes, and he fell back unconscious just as he prepared to emerge. Fortunately an assistant became aware of his predicament and hauled him out. Such unforeseeable accidents were rare with him, however, and in his opinion inexcusable. He was not a daring man in the sense his audience sometimes believed him to be; he was, instead, a cool, calculating, highly-trained technician. He worked hard on the stage; but he worked much harder behind it.

He was, for example, one of the greatest experts on handcuffs the world has ever known. Although he never attempted to claim that he had invented the handcuff release, nor any of its chain or rope-tie variations, he did contend—and fiercely—that he had developed the so-called challenge escape. Certainly his skill and his knowledge brought that particular type of escape to a peak of success never realized before or since. After that one early defeat at the hands of a

Chicago detective, he never again failed at any handcuff challenge his public could contrive. He *knew* handcuffs.

And when, in 1905, the number of his imitators—some of them quite successful—convinced him that he should win his future applause in other fields, he still found ways to make use of that knowledge for his own advancement and to the despair of his rivals. He published, in his *Monthly*, a series of articles explaining the mechanism of various cuffs, and how they might be opened. He stated, for example, that certain irons, including some of the British varieties, could be sprung by means of a brisk tap at one point. He described the use of common lockpicks, and presented, in text and illustration, many less common types. The result was to put a fairly effective end to the popularity of handcuff artists. Houdini had made information about their methods so easily available that almost anybody could become a cuff escapist of sorts.

But even so Houdini had not published everything he knew on the subject. A few years later, in 1908, he sold his remaining handcuff secrets through Roteberg, the Chicago magic dealer, under an arrangement by which Houdini received a royalty on all sales. The item included a booklet and a set of equipment; the instruction leaflet alone sold for five dollars, the complete act for thirty-five. And they went "like wildfire," according to Ralph Read, the youngster who had once helped the Houdinis to stage a "spirit show" in St. Joseph, Missouri, and who was by then handling Roteberg's mail-order business. "Hundreds bought only the secret instructions," Read declared, "so anxious were they to learn how the release was performed."

All of Houdini's escapes—and escapes of some variety comprised most of his material—can be roughly divided into two groups: the prepared escapes, and the challenges.

The former caused him no difficulty once he had stepped forth on the stage. Their difficulties had all been met and overcome beforehand in the workshop which Houdini's hotel room always became the minute he entered it. He and his ingenious assistants often worked there through the night. Houdini might be freeing himself simultaneously from half a dozen pairs of handcuffs, ten feet of chain, thirty feet of rope, and a securely locked and tied box—but the release was as easy as breathing for him if all the restraints were his own. The cuffs and padlocks he used as "window dressing" could be opened by pressure on a tiny pin. His packing cases, trunks, and other containers had sliding panels or other carefully concealed devices by means of which he could instantly extricate himself. Of course, all of these "fakes," as they are known in the profession, were planned and executed with consummate skill. No committee from the audience ever discovered their secrets. Houdini was constantly discarding tricks because he suspected that some one of his fellow-performers had guessed how a certain "fake" was contrived.

Houdini's Escapes and Magic, by Walter B. Gibson, explains many of Houdini's tricks and describes much of his equipment, but even this thick volume does not tell the whole story. Gibson, a magician himself, did not permit Gibson, the author, to expose tricks still in use at the time of the book's publication. And, furthermore, Houdini's notes, from which the book was compiled, were not in themselves complete— because he trusted his memory, or because he trusted no one else, Houdini sometimes failed to explain a trick completely even in the privacy of his own notebooks. But we know enough about his effects today to recognize that he was as brilliant an inventor as he was a showman.

His prepared escapes were, however, only his bread-and-butter work: they might demand great physical strength and dexterity, extraordinary stamina and skill, but they presented him with no special problem once they were ready for the stage. His challenge escapes were another matter altogether. And his spectacular success at meeting and defeating so many hundreds of these challenges, of such infinite variety, attests to the remarkable mental and physical ability which Houdini brought to his role as performer.

"He *can't* get out of this box. I made it myself of the toughest wood and the hardest nails I could find. There's no *way* for him to get out, once the lid's nailed down." That statement or a similar one referring to some other kind of restraint, was made in almost every major European and American city during the days of Houdini's career—but every man who spoke it was proved to be wrong. Houdini always got out.

A challenge escape could not be prepared for, in the sense that the prepared escape was planned, worked out, and rehearsed before presentation. But it nevertheless demanded an enormous amount of preparation. Part of this consisted simply of Houdini's own wide knowledge, and the additional knowledge of such clever assistants as Franz Kukol, who was with him for twenty years, and James Collins and James Vickery, both of whom served him for nearly as long. All four men could guess ahead of time, and pretty accurately, just what problems each challenge would present. Those who sought to hold Houdini in some novel restraint were experts in their own line; Houdini and his staff were experts in many lines.

But expert knowledge alone was not enough. Houdini also usually required a certain amount of time to put his knowledge to use. Thus he accepted the challenge one evening, and performed the test itself a night or two later.

In the case of handcuffs or fetters, the challenger was asked to bring the articles with him to the stage, so that Houdini might see them before formally accepting the challenge. He was seldom presented with a cuff or fetter that he had not seen before. More often than not, his own extensive collection included a duplicate of the restraint the challenger believed to be so unusual. And even on those rare occasions when Houdini did encounter a novel fetter of some sort, his practised eye required but a moment to probe its secret, and his trained mind but little longer to choose or contrive the lockpick that would open the mechanism.

Much of Houdini's success depended upon lockpicks, ingeniously made and just as ingeniously concealed, either on his person or in some other accessible spot. Some of the ones he used were extremely simple; others were amazingly complicated; almost all of them were miraculously small.

As an example, the regulation British cuff of the period had a special keyhole. This keyhole was plugged with a screw after the cuff had been locked on the prisoner's wrists. To release this cuff Houdini devised a minute mechanism consisting in part of a tiny wheel. He could operate it with two fingers of one hand, or—by holding the pick in his teeth—turn the small wheel with his tongue. Another pick was fitted with extension arms and gears, so that he could utilize it even when, as often happened, his hands were held some distance apart by a rigid bar separating the two cuffs. And he used a simple strip of hard steel, made to meticulous measurements, to open the ratchet cuff popular in the United States.

Possession of a lockpick did not of course mean that releasing himself from cruel and intricate fetters was necessarily easy. His bodily agility, his muscular strength, and the great dexterity of his toes and fingers were all vital to him. He needed the picks *in addition* to those factors. And he took as much care to see that his picks and other tools were available and usable, as he did to keep himself in bodily trim. The chair that stood inside his cabinet was therefore no ordinary chair—and different ones were used for differing circumstances. One such article of apparently innocent furniture had a slotted leg into which a pick could be inserted. Then if Houdini could not use his hands to pick the lock, he could by contorting his body into the proper position, bring the troublesome manacles into contact with the pick. A hollow post of the cabinet itself might be similarly used or might serve to conceal the lockpick until it was needed.

Houdini was aware, of course, that he would occasionally, and despite all his precautions, be faced with unfair challenges: plugged cuffs, fetters that had been soaked in water so that their interior mechanism had been rusted fast, cuffs whose keys were deliberately snapped off inside the lock at the time they were fastened to the performer's wrists or ankles. Houdini's public boast was that he would attempt to release himself only from those fetters which had not been "doctored"; nevertheless, he hated to refuse any challenge at all: the public might think the fault was his rather than his challenger's. Consequently, he devised special cabinets to be used when— and only when—he found himself face to face with these special problems. Each of these cabinets, although subject to the usual examination by an audience committee, was capable of concealing an assistant who would help Houdini free himself from any cuff, no matter how artfully "fixed."

One such cabinet was roofed with a canopy supported by iron rods; and because the cabinet was fairly high and wide, the canopy itself— though clearly consisting of two separated layers of material—seemed so shallow that no one suspected it offered a place of concealment. To further insure himself against exposure by some particularly curious and agile committeeman, who might conceivably climb one of those poles to explore the canopy, Houdini had the supporting rods lightly coated with grease; committeemen, he knew, were not likely to carry on their investigations under conditions ruinous to their clothes and their dignity.

It was not Houdini, the inventor, who greased those poles; it was Houdini, the showman, the man who knew his audience as well as he knew the mechanical techniques of his trade. That same knowledge of the audience was a useful tool in the art of misdirection—an art which Houdini frequently called to his aid when technical means were not enough.

Although he always denied that it was possible—for him or anyone else—to compress the hands to so small a compass that a cuff locked on the wrists could be slid down over them, effecting a release without unlocking the cuffs at all, he did occasionally manage to do just that. But he did it by a skilful ruse, skilfully managed. Thus, when he was challenged to escape from a fetter for which he had no pick, and for which he could not —usually because there was no time—prepare one, his immediate reaction was to complain that the fetter was too easy to offer him a worthwhile challenge. He would thereupon recommend that the challenger increase the difficulty of the performance; let him, Houdini would suggest, add several other manacles to the test. Such manacles were immediately brought forward by Houdini's assistants and—to the challenger's admiration— affixed to Houdini's forearms, from the wrist up.

The challenger's own handcuffs were then locked on above them.

Smothered in irons, from his wrists to his elbows, Houdini seemed indeed securely restrained. But it was, of course, a matter of seconds before he had removed the lower cuffs, all of which were from his own collection. He was then left with only the challenger's cuffs, and now these no longer bothered him. They had been locked around the upper arm and could therefore, though the effort might cost Houdini several inches of scraped skin, be slipped down to the smaller circumference of the wrist and over the tightly squeezed hands.

Misdirection also offered the solution to many of the problems posed by the need to conceal his lockpicks. Although Houdini himself never said so, it is clear that he managed to escape from certain prison cells by concealing his pick ahead of time somewhere within the cell—although it, too, was customarily searched, as was Houdini's person. He did say that once, at least, he had taped a lockpick to the sole of his foot before he was shut into a cell; he had discovered that that was one place which was seldom examined.

Probably, too, he often moved the pick from one place to another while the search was being made, shifting it by deft sleight of hand from his mouth to his palm and then to his hair, after each of those parts of his body had already been examined. And it is probable that he used the skill he had learned from the "swallowers" encountered in his dime museum days, to conceal temporarily one of the small objects on which his success depended. In one of his escapes he actually slipped his lockpick beneath the coat collar of one of his searchers—and retrieved it later as he was being led, nude, into his cell.

Whatever means he used—and they must have been varied—one thing seems certain: Houdini opened those thousands of fetters and prison locks by his own skill, wits, and dexterity alone. There was never the slightest hint of connivance with officials. He was given far too many endorsements and certificates by incorruptible police chiefs to doubt that.

Each type of challenge escape presented its own problems. In extricating himself from rope ties, for example, Houdini ordinarily depended entirely upon his strength and agility, and his knowledge of ropes and of his challengers. Invariably he invited the latter to use as much rope as they liked—because he was aware that when, say, sixty feet of rope were to be knotted and bound around him, the first few knots would be securely fashioned, but that eventually his opponent would tire, and the remaining length would be carelessly and hastily tied. Afterward, in his cabinet, only those first few knots would give Houdini any serious trouble. When his hands had been tied behind his back he could, by sheer strength, force the arms down until they were behind his knees; then he would sit on the floor, and one after the other, slip his legs through so that his hands were before his face, and their knots could be tackled with the aid of sight and teeth. He also invited his challengers to use the heaviest rope they wished, especially for securing his feet—because he knew that the heavier the rope, the less tight the knots, and that very tight knots might be impossible to untie even for his highly educated toes. One of the most difficult rope challenges he ever had to meet was done with fine light fishline.

When he suspected that agility and strength would not serve his purpose, Houdini employed some of the secrets of his trade. "If the committee begins to make more knots than suits you," he wrote in his account of rope ties for other magicians, "it will be well to swell the muscles, expand the chest, slightly hunch the shoulders, and hold the arms a little away from the sides. . . . You should always wear a coat when submitting to this tie, as that will be found to be an added help in obtaining the slack. . . . Just as with the strait jacket, it becomes necessary to gain the first slack. It may be done by misguiding the tier or by main muscular strength of the tied. In either case, once secured, the escape can be effectually made."

And if the knots were, despite all his wiles, too numerous or too difficult to be untied within a reasonable period, Houdini did not hesitate to make use of the knife hidden on his person or in his cabinet. If it was necessary to sever the rope in several places, Houdini was ready with a substitute that he had previously wrapped around his body under his clothes; if he had cut only a few inches from the challenger's rope, he reappeared with the original, calmly confident that its shortened length would never be suspected. The cut pieces, of course, he hid before he emerged.

Houdini knew that certain variations of the rope tie—notably the one done with wet sheets, the knots of which were almost impossible to undo—demanded more of his skill and dexterity than almost any other challenge he ever accepted. In the eyes of the spectators, however, several of his escapes from his challengers' containers seemed far more miraculous. These containers, contrived by the skilled and ingenious workmen of a dozen countries, included such seemingly indestructible objects as heavy timber packing cases, steel boxes, and iron boilers; and such fragile articles as glass boxes, cardboard cartons, wicker hampers, and paper bags. Houdini had to extricate himself from the latter group without noticeable harm to the container. The apparently-unbreakable restraint and the all-too-easily-broken one each presented their own difficulties, although Houdini's methods for both were based on similar principles.

For all these escapes—as for those involving handcuffs—the challengers were asked to bring their restraint to the theater at the time the challenge was formally made and accepted. Houdini then asked—and the request seemed reasonable enough—that the container itself be left at the theater for the purposes of display until the performance of the test, usually scheduled for the following evening. He explained that the challengers would have ample time and opportunity for re-examination of the object before the trial took place, to assure themselves that it had not been tampered with during the interval. The challengers always agreed to his stipulation; a lobby exhibit was, after all, exactly the sort of personal publicity they expected for their defiance of the Escape King.

When challenged by the employes of a boiler factory—to take an oft-repeated example—those employes could watch their securely riveted boiler being admired in the lobby during all the hours the theater was open that day and the next. They could listen to people comment on the skill with which the top of the boiler was secured to the body by means of long steel rods, piercing the lid and padlocked into position. They could pride themselves on the conclusion reached by their fellow townspeople—the conclusion that Houdini would certainly never escape from this iron cylinder once he had been locked inside.

But what the challengers didn't know, and what they apparently never suspected, was that when the theater was closed for the night their boiler was hastily removed to Houdini's dressing room, where it was subjected to subtle and invisible change. First its padlocks would be opened —by whatever lockpick seemed most suitable for the job—and the steel bars would be lifted out. These were then replaced with other bars, which —although they did not appear to differ from the original—were actually made of a very soft type of iron. The padlocks were then put back on, and the boiler was ready for the performance.

Houdini's challengers would mount the stage when the crucial moment had come, study their boiler carefully and—since none of them was ever shrewd enough to test those bars with a file or hacksaw—declare that it had clearly not been touched since it left their hands. Houdini would step inside, the lid would be put on, the bars padlocked in place, the cabinet curtains drawn around it, and the orchestra would burst into a loud—a rather unusually loud—selection. Under cover of that sound Houdini would swiftly cut through the bars by means of the thin blade he had hidden on his person. Once severed, the bars were pushed up and through the lid, to fall with only a slight thud on the heavily carpeted cabinet floor. Houdini would then lift the lid, crawl out, replace the top—and insert the *original* steel rods, concealed until then in the cabinet's hollow supports. A moment later, having hidden the severed soft rods in those same supports, together with the tiny iron filings which might otherwise give him away, he was ready to step out of his cabinet, once more victorious.

One of the escapes, described in *The Secrets of Houdini* by J. C. Cannell, was made from a box constructed of iron one-eighth of an inch thick with a heavy lid secured by four bolts fastened with nuts and cotterpins. When the lid was in place Houdini was to push those bolts through, from the inside; the committee would then tighten the nuts and insert the pins. The test went off as scheduled, and Houdini was, of course, successful; it had been, for him, a particularly easy escape. Houdini had hidden on himself a duplicate set of bolts, made in such a way that their heads could be removed from the inside; these he pushed through to the challengers, and these were fastened by the pins. Houdini then unscrewed their heads, pushed up the bolts, and lifted the lid. Once outside he attached strings to the real bolts, leaving them inside the box but pulling the ends of the strings through the holes in the lid, put the lid in place, pulled the bolts through, fastened the nuts, and inserted the pins. Then he hid the fake bolts—and was done.

Escaping from a huge paper bag was no more difficult; but it was equally effective because Houdini's showmanship precluded the one obvious possibility—that he had simply ripped it open and, before his reappearance, substituted for it another sealed bag of identical proportions and material. To assure his audience that he had not perpetrated such a substitution, he always asked all members of the challenging group, plus the members of a volunteer audience committee, to inscribe their names or initials on the bag just before the top of it was sealed over his head. And to reproduce all those names and initials in the brief moment during which the curtains of Houdini's cabinet were drawn was clearly beyond even his near-miraculous powers. Actually all that Houdini did, in order to effect his escape, was to cut the top of the bag off just below the gummed edge. Once outside, he cut a new flap and sealed it in place with the adhesive he had at hand. It was the same psychology he applied to some of his rope escapes: the loss of a few inches from the bag's seven-foot height was simply never noticed.

One of Houdini's most spectacular challenge escapes—and a dramatic example of the ease with which he overcame a seemingly insuperable obstacle—occurred when he was playing at London's great Euston Palace. Houdini had announced that he would attempt an escape from any bank safe in England, and a challenge had been forthcoming, not from an individual bank, but from a bank-vault manufacturer who had recently completed the construction of a new vault believed to be utterly impenetrable. Houdini accepted—with the usual and never refused condition that the challenger's container be brought to the theater twenty-four hours before the test.

The theater was jammed on the night of the trial: both the theater manager and the vault manufacturer had promised the public a conclusive test of Houdini's powers. And when the audience saw the massive vault on the stage—the foundations had had to be reinforced to accommodate its weight—it too felt that this event would settle once and for all Houdini's ability to escape from any restraint man was capable of contriving. The vault was examined by the manufacturer's experts and by a committee from the audience; all agreed that it was in the same condition in which it had left the factory, and that its lock was certainly impervious to manipulation from within. Houdini was examined by a doctor and declared to be without aids or instruments of any kind on his person.

The performer then made a brief impressive speech to the audience, explaining to them how little air would be available within the locked

vault, and that he would have to escape quickly
if he were to live to escape at all. Finally Houdini
shook hands solemnly with the entire committee,
thanking them for their zeal and thoroughness,
and—looking particularly slight and helpless in
the bathing suit he wore (beneath which, the
audience realized, it would have been impossible
to conceal an implement of any sort)—he
stepped into the great vault, and the door was
swung shut and locked behind him. A screen was
placed around the vault, so that no one—no assistant of Houdini's, that is—might approach it
without being detected. The audience and the
committee began their watchful vigil.

Fifteen minutes crept slowly by, and then another five. Faint nervous murmurs began to be
heard from the expectant crowd. At the end of
half an hour a considerable number of the spectators had broken the heavy silence to call out
that Houdini be released—that he would die for
lack of air if the door were not opened. But Houdini's assistants, although making it clear that
they too shared the tenseness of the atmosphere,
insisted that they had been ordered not to request
an unlocking of the safe until they heard a pre-
arranged signal of distress from the King of
Escapists.

When forty minutes had passed, most of the
women in the vast audience were clamorously
demanding Houdini's liberation. He no longer

had the strength, they said, to give the awaited signal. The committee conferred helplessly; they didn't want to be responsible for Houdini's death, and yet on the other hand. . . .

At the expiration of forty-five minutes the audience was in an uproar—and at that moment Houdini walked serenely out from behind the curtains.

While the hundreds of applauding men and women screamed and shouted their admiration, the vault manufacturer's representative opened the heavy door with the one available key—which had been in his possession during the entire period of waiting—and announced in a shaken and wondering voice that neither the door itself nor the lock had been tampered with.

The vault escape was one of Houdini's greatest triumphs, and he had earned it—although not quite by the means the audience might have imagined. He had, in a sense, begun to make his escape from the massive box the night before. It was then, in his workroom, that he had taken apart the lock's mechanism and replaced strong springs with weak ones. The new springs worked as well as the old when the vault's key was used, but they enabled the lock to be opened from the inside by a slender lockpick.

On the night of the test, Houdini's only problem was to obtain that lockpick, and he did it by a simple ruse. One of the members of the committee was his friend and fellow-magician, Will Goldston; and when Houdini shook hands with him, as he made his solemn round of the group, Houdini palmed the pick from Goldston's hand where it had been attached to the inner side of a ring. He was therefore able to open the vault almost the instant he was locked inside. Then he sat reading quietly behind the cabinet curtains until he felt the audience had reached the exact pitch of excitement which would make his reappearance most effective. Later that night, of course, the vault's lock was removed a second time, and the original springs reinserted; the vault manufacturer had no evidence whatsoever of the means by which Houdini had managed his escape.

Success was the single, almost-unvarying factor in his career, together with a stubborn determination which drove him to any conceivable lengths to achieve that success. The methods he used were various; the tricks he devised and practised were without number. But all of them demanded an infinite attention to detail, constant exertion of nervous and physical energy, and endless hours of thought, training, and rehearsal. Houdini was willing to pay that price over and over again for the position of leadership it earned him, and for the satisfaction of maintaining that leadership.

The elaborate bronze bust of his own design

erected at his own orders over Houdini's grave, is
a monument to the man's vanity rather than to
the man himself. But he has his own living monument on the lips of all who still use his name—
use it as a synonym for the strength and skill that
laugh at handcuffs, for the courage and independence that cannot be bound by any fetters in
the world.

INDEX

INDEX

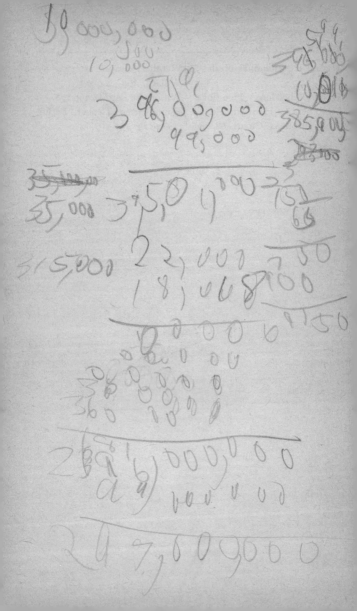